BOOK LUST
TO GO

BOOK LUST
TO GO

NANCY PEARL

RECOMMENDED READING FOR TRAVELERS, VAGABONDS, AND DREAMERS

SASQUATCH BOOKS
SEATTLE

Printed in the United States of America
Published by Sasquatch Books
Distributed by PGW/Perseus
15 14 13 12 11 10   9 8 7 6 5 4 3 2 1

Cover photograph: Clare Barboza
Cover map: © iStockphoto.com/belterz/vintage map
Cover design: Rosebud Eustace
Interior maps: © Map Resources
Interior design: Rowan Moore-Seifred
Interior composition: Sarah Plein

Library of Congress Cataloging-in-Publication Data

Pearl, Nancy.
  Book lust to go : recommended reading for travelers, vagabonds, and dreamers / Nancy Pearl.
      p. cm.
  Includes bibliographical references and index.
  ISBN-13: 978-1-57061-650-1
  ISBN-10: 1-57061-650-7
  1. Travel--Bibliography. 2. Best books. I. Title.
  Z6004.T6P39 2010
  011.6--dc22

                              2010020633

Sasquatch Books
119 South Main Street, Suite 400
Seattle, WA 98104
(206) 467-4300
www.sasquatchbooks.com
custserv@sasquatchbooks.com

SUSTAINABLE FORESTRY INITIATIVE Certified Fiber Sourcing
Label applies to the text stock www.sfiprogram.org

Contents

GEOGRAPHICAL INDEX

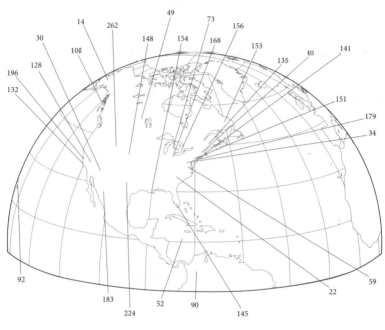

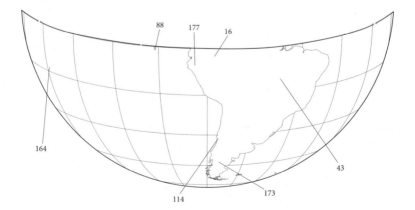

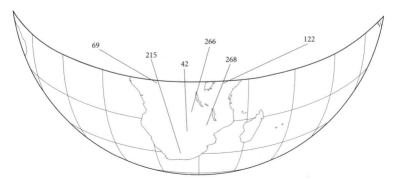

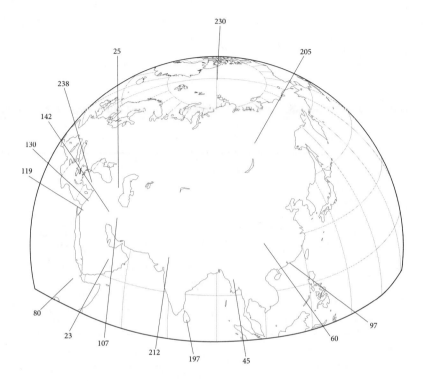

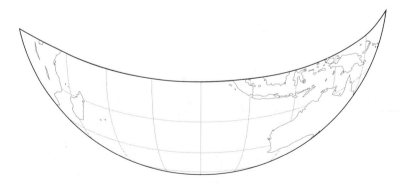

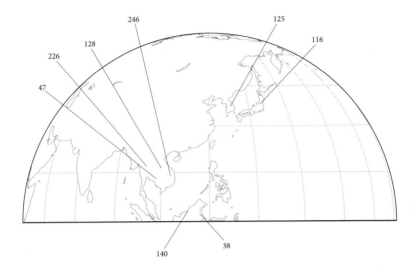

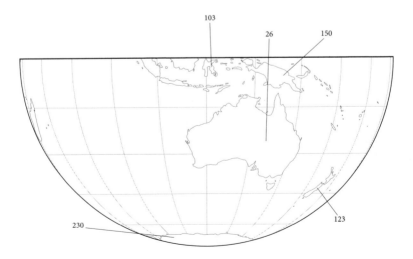

INTRODUCTION

I am not an enthusiastic traveler. Let me lay my cards on the table, clear the air, call a spade a spade, and make something perfectly clear. I am barely a traveler at all. I would like to attribute this to "The Unexplorer," a poem by Edna St. Vincent Millay that I read when I was about thirteen and deeply into poetry. It's from her collection called **A Few Figs from Thistles** and is a whole novel in six short lines, all about a young girl enraptured by the road outside her house. When she asks her mother about it, she's told that the road "led to the milkman's door." Millay concludes with the line: "(That's why I have not traveled more.)"

And then I've always feared that what Ralph Waldo Emerson said in **Self-Reliance** is true:

> Traveling is a fool's paradise . . . I pack my trunk, embrace my friends, embark on the sea and at last wake up in Naples, and there beside me is the stern fact, the sad self, unrelenting, identical, that I fled from.

But to blame that sort of literary disillusionment for my lack of travel would be romantic in the extreme, and also highly disingenuous. Here's why I don't travel: I am stymied by the very activities of planning a trip and figuring out an itinerary, choosing dates and what to pack. I am frustrated by my inability to speak any language except English. My high school French just won't cut it. You try finding a Laundromat in Tallinn without knowing Estonian and you'll soon discover that although everyone has assured you that all Estonians speak at least a rudimentary form of English, that doesn't really seem to apply to most people over thirty. I don't blame them for not speaking English; I blame myself for not speaking Estonian so I could explain that I just wanted to wash my dirty clothes.

I am also made anxious by the seemingly simple act of leaving my house. I can manage meeting friends for coffee, going for walks in my familiar neighborhood, and geocaching. But even that last activity, as much as I enjoy being with my geocaching buddies, is more often than not nerve-wracking in the extreme as we drive to and disembark in unfamiliar locales all around the city. That's about it, travelwise, for me.

In his book **Between Terror and Tourism**, Michael Mewshaw writes of arriving in a totally inhospitable desert locale: "The pleasure of being where I had never been before, doing what I had never done, bound for who knew what—I found it all thrilling. I always have."

And I have not, alas.

So in one way of looking at it, I am totally the wrong person to write a book about travel; on the other hand, I am absolutely the perfect person. I am, in fact, a virtual traveler, via books. I have always loved reading armchair travel books and accounts of dashing and daring explorers. I adore books—whether fiction or nonfiction—that give me a sense of being in another place and time. There are so many wonderful books that do exactly that; it was the impetus for *Book Lust To Go.* The first thing I did when I started working on this book was to purchase a large and up-to-date world map and put it up on the wall of the room where I write, so it was easy for me to get up from my desk, look at where a country or city was located, and understand its political and geographical context. It's probably one of the best purchases I've ever made.

Now for some information about what's in this book (and what's not).

First, as with the other three books in the Book Lust series, I've included titles that are both in print and out of print. Honestly, I wish they were all in print and easily available at libraries and bookstores. We're lucky in this age of the Internet that many out-of-print books are easy to locate and purchase online. And you can take advantage of the inter-library loan service most libraries offer their patrons.

Second, I've included my favorite armchair travel narratives, as well as biographies of explorers, memoirs, novels set in various countries around the world, and a smattering of history. I hope they'll become your favorites as well, whether you're a virtual or actual traveler.

Third, *Book Lust*, published in 2003, and *More Book Lust*, which came out in 2005, featured lots of titles that would have fit wonderfully into *Book Lust To Go*. If I had ever imagined that I would write a Book Lust series, I might have saved them to include here, but I never saw that coming (nor, I think, did anyone else). I have generally chosen not to repeat titles here, except when one seemed especially well suited for *Book Lust To Go*. So before you email me about a title or an author that you're concerned I've omitted from *Book Lust To Go*, be sure to check my other books first!

One of my favorite discoveries while I was doing all of the preliminary reading for *BLTG* (as I affectionately refer to it) was reading

Josie Dew's memoir **A Ride in the Neon Sun**. Here's what she says about traveling:

> Some people travel with firm ideas for a journey, following in the footsteps of an intrepid ancestor whose exotic exploits were happened upon in a dusty, cobweb-laced attic containing immovable trunks full of sepia-curled daguerreotypes and age-discoloured letters redolent of bygone days. Others travel for anthropological, botanical, archaeological, geological, and other logical reasons. Some are smitten by a specific country brewed from childhood dreams. For others, travel is a challenge, a release, an escape, a shaking off of the shackles, and even if they don't know where they will end up they usually know where they will begin.

The very hardest part of writing this book was that I was unable to stop working on it. I kept reading even after the initial manuscript was turned in, discovering new titles and authors whose works I just couldn't bear to leave out. I even envisioned myself watching the book being printed and shouting periodically, "Stop the presses!" so that I could add yet another section or title. But of course the day actually came when I knew I had to stop or there would never be an end to the project. And here is the result, in your hands right now.

So, before your next trip—either virtual or actual—grab a pen and begin making notes about the titles that sound good to you. And enjoy the journeys.

I'd love to hear from you. My email address is nancy@nancypearl .com.

ACKNOWLEDGMENTS

Many people gave me great suggestions for books to include in *Book Lust To Go*. I want to give an especial shout-out to Martha Bayley, who actually kick-started the whole process of me really sitting down and writing up all my notes; in addition, she contributed both the "Inside the Inside Passage" section and "We'll Always Have Paris." She is herself both a virtual and actual traveler, and over the years has recommended many terrific books. And Anna Minard, who initially organized my reams of random bits of paper—something I never could have done on my own—into a coherent arrangement.

And to all these folks for their help of many different sorts:

Nassim Assefi; Jen Baker; Abby Bass; Colleen Brady; Brad Craft; Marilyn Dahl; Beth de la Fuente; Janneke Dijkstra; Jason Felton; Margaret Ford; Gitana Garofalo; Gail Goodrick; Andrea Gough; Alex Harris; Phyllis Hatfield; Jim Horton; Christine Jeffords; Linda Johns; Mark Kaiser; Kathleen Kinder; Bharti Kirschner; David Laskin; Mike Leber; Susan Linn; Lisa Lundström; Nancy McGill; Cindy Mitchell; Gina Nahai; Hannah Parker; Eily Raman; Gayle Richardson; Matt Rowe; Cadi Russell-Sauve; Robin Pforr Ryan; Murray Sampson; Anne Schwendiman; Jake Silverstein; Kale Sniderman; Stephen and Marilyn Sniderman; Shoshana Sniderman-Wise; Dana Stabenow; Manya and Pär Sundstrom; Martha Tofferi; Jason Vanhee; Agnes Wiacek; David Wright; Neal Wyatt (for the "Anglophile's Literary Pilgrimage," "Comics with a Sense of Place," and "Lyme Regis" sections, and who is always as excited about my books as I am); and Michelle Young.

I apologize in advance if I've inadvertently omitted your name....

And all my thanks to the wonderful folks at Sasquatch Books—it takes a concerted togetherness to get a book from an idea to the printed page, and everyone at Sasquatch has been nothing less than supportive, especially Gary Luke, Sarah Hanson, Rachelle Longé, Tess Tabor, and Shari Miranda.

As always, love to my husband, Joe, to whom I owe more than I can say—he makes everything I do possible and makes possible everything that I do.

This book is dedicated to my granddaughter Jessica Pearl Raman, because it's her turn and I love her.

A IS FOR ADVENTURE

Any sort of adventurous travel comes with an almost guaranteed risk: anything can—and often does—go wrong, whether it's bad weather, bad decisions, bad karma, or simply bad luck. In addition to the best-selling armchair adventure titles by authors like Jon Krakauer, Sebastian Junger, or Linda Greenlaw, try these riveting accounts.

In **Adrift** by Steven Callahan, the author must use his inflatable life raft after his small sloop capsized after less than a week out on the open waters of the North Atlantic. The seventy-six days at sea that he spent fighting for his life and his sanity make for a spellbinding tale.

A Voyage for Madmen by Peter Nichols is about the first Golden Globe Race in 1968, in which—as the book's tagline has it—"Nine men set out to race each other around the world. Only one made it back." I read with a growing sense of shock—and no little admiration—how these men, for various and sundry reasons, decided to risk their bodies (and their minds) to take part in a race sans GPS, sans mobile phones, and in boats that seemed all but guaranteed not to survive the trip. Chay Blyth, who had very little experience in open water sailing, describes the end of his race when his boat became unmanageable during an unseasonable gale:

> So I lowered the sails . . . and once I had lowered
> them there was nothing more I could do except
> pray. So I prayed. And between times I turned to
> one of my sailing manuals to see what advice it
> contained for me. It was like being in hell with
> instructions.

Jeffrey Tayler's **River of No Reprieve: Descending Siberia's Waterway of Exile, Death, and Destiny** and **Murderers in Mausoleums: Riding the Back Roads of Empire Between Moscow and Beijing** both showcase the author's talents as a travel writer: powers of keen observation and an ability to convey his own palpable enthusiasm for exotic places and interesting people, even as danger is always just around the corner.

Many people make the choice to set off on an adventure, but the men described in Dean King's **Skeletons on the Zahara: A True Story of Survival** merely ended up where they did by accident. In August of 1815, twelve crew members from the Connecticut merchant brig *Commerce* were shipwrecked off the western coast of Africa, enslaved by a Bedouin tribe, and forced to accompany their captors—by foot and by camelback—on a seemingly endless, desperately grueling, and bone-dry trek through the sands of the western Sahara desert (now part of Morocco). King based his book on two first-person accounts of the experience the men underwent; from these two works, King has constructed a gripping and page-turning narrative of survival and courage. The fact that as this story was unfolding alongside a parallel story of survival and courage in the face of dire circumstances—the abduction and enslavement in the "New World" of African native men, women, and children—makes King's book especially ironic.

Deep-sea diving off the coast of French Polynesia: could anything be more, well, um, adventurous? Not according to Julia Whitty in **The Fragile Edge: Diving and Other Adventures in the South Pacific**.

James West Davidson and John Rugge's **Great Heart: The History of a Labrador Adventure** chronicles the story of a failed exploration that was dogged with bad luck, as well as its complicated aftermath.

Mumbai to Mecca: A Pilgrimage to the Holy Sites of Islam by Ilija Trojanow (his name is also spelled Ilya Troyanov—see the section called "Star Trekkers" for another of his books) is one of the bound-to-be-classic travelogues: an account of the Hajj as seen through the eyes of a Western journalist sympathetic to Islam.

I enjoyed so many of the selections Lamar Underwood collected in **The Greatest Adventure Stories Ever Told**. They include both fiction and nonfiction, from an Arthur Conan Doyle non-Sherlockian short story and Tom Wolfe's account of Chuck Yeager's breaking the sound barrier, to a short story by Arthur C. Clarke and Joel P. Kramer's "A Harrowing Journey," which describes a trip (by foot and kayak) through New Guinea that seemed so desperately foolhardy I found myself wincing in sympathetic pain while I was reading it.

AFGHANISTAN: GRAVEYARD OF EMPIRES

As with many of the places I've included in this book, probably the only way we're going to get to visit Afghanistan (unless we're in the military) in the next few years is through the books we read. I somehow doubt that most of us will be making vacation plans to visit Kabul. But who knows? You may be far more adventurous than I.

The only positive outcome of the events of 9/11 that I can see is the proliferation of books—both fiction and nonfiction—set in a country that most of us never before paid much attention to. I wrote a whole section in *More Book Lust* that covers fiction and nonfiction about Afghanistan's past and present, and you might want to begin there. But, to quote Lewis Carroll's "The Walrus and the Carpenter" on the subject of oysters, "And thick and fast they came at last / And more and more and more." It's true, as all you observant readers have already gathered by now, that this is not a section that's going to provide a lot of laughs. On the other hand, most of these books are perfect selections for your book group. But do me one favor—read these in the spring (or summer) of the year. They aren't—for the most part—the best choice for gray and rainy days.

Nonfiction

One of the best books I read in 2009 (although perhaps "experienced" is a better choice of verb) was the graphic novel **The Photographer: Into War-Torn Afghanistan with Doctors Without Borders** by Emmanuel Guibert, Didier Lefèvre, and Frédéric Lemercier. It's the powerful story of Lefèvre's first assignment as a photojournalist in 1986, accompanying a team of Médecins sans Frontières (Doctors Without Borders) who were traveling through Pakistan to Afghanistan, during the long bloody conflict between the invading Soviet Union troops and the Taliban. The pictures include both Lefèvre's original contact sheets (it's interesting to note that contact sheets of photos are not unlike strips of comics) and Guibert's drawings, while the text is reconstructed from discussions Guibert and Lefèvre had about the journey. Graphic designer Lemercier assembled the book. (Lefèvre's journals—mentioned in the book—were lost years before.)

Other good reading choices:

Saira Shah's **The Storyteller's Daughter: One Woman's Return to Her Lost Homeland** weaves tales that Shah heard growing up in Britain with her own impressions during a long sojourn in country. Shah is also a highly regarded filmmaker, whose documentary *Beneath the Veil: Inside the Taliban's Afghanistan* is disturbing and necessary viewing for anyone interested in understanding the country. As is her book.

In his **Opium Season: A Year on the Afghan Frontier**, Joel Hafvenstein describes the year he spent working with an American aid organization to try to help Afghani farmers raise crops other than those that have been their livelihood for generations.

Seth G. Jones's **In the Graveyard of Empires: America's War in Afghanistan** provides an excellent history of U.S. involvement in the country.

One of the earliest books written about the battle between the Russian invaders and the mujahideen fighters is **Under a Sickle Moon: A Journey Through Afghanistan**. In 1984 Peregrine Hodson, a British freelance journalist, traveled with the resistance fighters throughout northeastern Afghanistan. His book is not, as Hodson makes clear in his introduction, an analysis of the war or the politics of the region. But reading it now, more than twenty years after it was originally published, one finds familiar names throughout, and the beginnings of stories that are not yet ended.

In **The Places In Between**, Rory Stewart describes a trip through Afghanistan shortly after the fall of the Taliban, early in 2002. Having spent much of 2000 and 2001 trekking across Iran, Pakistan, India, and Nepal, Stewart decided to walk from Herat to Kabul. He followed the route of Babur, a fifteenth-century leader best known as the founder of the Mughal Empire, and took with him only his dog, who was named for this most famous emperor. Canine lovers take note: Babur is one of the best dogs in literature.

J. Malcolm Garcia's **The Khaarijee: A Chronicle of Friendship and War in Kabul** is the story of a middle-aged newbie reporter who cuts his teeth in the heat of Afghanistan following 9/11.

Jon Krakauer's **Where Men Win Glory: The Odyssey of Pat Tillman** is the moving account of the great pro football player's death in Afghanistan. As with all of Krakauer's books, this is eminently readable.

Fiction

Most readers are already familiar with Khaled Hosseini's two novels, **The Kite Runner** and **A Thousand Splendid Suns**. (In fact, those are the two works of fiction that probably introduced many readers to Afghanistan.) But don't stop there—here are others you shouldn't miss:

Nadeem Aslam's **The Wasted Vigil**; Dan Fesperman's **The Warlord's Son** (especially good for John le Carré fans); James Michener's **Caravans**, which animates the 1940s and 1950s in Afghanistan quite marvelously; and Atiq Rahimi's **The Patience Stone**, which helps us understand the role and place of Afghani women. (The introduction to Rahimi's novel was written by Khaled Hosseini.)

AFRICA: THE GREENEST CONTINENT

I think it was Graham Greene who called Africa "the greenest continent." Given the size and complexity of the continent, I could probably do a whole *Book Lust To Go* volume on books about Africa, which would only befit a locale that is 11.7 million square miles and comprises, according to Wikipedia, sixty-one political territories and fifty-three different countries, many of which are probably unfamiliar to the western reader (or at least to this particular western reader). Books about Africa can be arranged into enough categories to make even the most discerning slicer and dicer content (or queasy). Many of the titles cross categories.

There are the BYH ("break your heart") books that range from history to classic fiction (**Cry the Beloved Country** by Alan Paton, for one) to contemporary mysteries (like Malla Nunn's **A Beautiful Place to Die** and Kwei Quartey's **Wife of the Gods**).

There are the older but still good police procedural mysteries by James McClure, featuring the white Inspector Kramer and his Zulu assistant, Zondi, that take place in South Africa during the long years of apartheid; **The Steam Pig** is my favorite.

There are the RCG ("rose-colored glasses") memoirs (like Isak Dinesen's **Out of Africa**) and the DFCiASSaCoO ("dysfunctional families come in all sizes, shapes, and countries of origin") autobiographies like **Don't Let's Go to the Dogs Tonight: An**

African Childhood by Alexandra Fuller. (There's more by this author in the "Zambia" section.)

I could go on for pages about the terrifyingly sad political accounts of bravery, pain, atrocities, and, unaccountably, hope, as they appear in recent nonfiction about Africa: Dave Eggers's **What Is the What**; **They Poured Fire on Us from the Sky: The True Story of Three Lost Boys from Sudan** by Alephfonsion Deng, Benson Deng, and Banjamin Ajak; Emmanuel Jal's **War Child**; Philip Gourevitch's **We Wish to Inform You That Tomorrow We Will Be Killed with Our Families: Stories from Rwanda** (you can watch my interview with Gourevitch at www.seattlechannel.org/videos/video.asp?ID=3030904); **A Thousand Hills: Rwanda's Rebirth and the Man Who Dreamed It** by Stephen Kinzer; Tracy Kidder's **Strength in What Remains** (see my interview with him at www.seattlechannel.org/videos/video.asp?ID=3031003); and Michela Wrong's **It's Our Turn to Eat: The Story of a Kenyan Whistle-Blower**.

It's true that many of these books don't necessarily make you want to get up and vacation in any of the continent's war-torn and depleted countries like Sudan, Somalia, or Rwanda (although reading the charming novel **Baking Cakes in Kigali** by Gaile Parkin might change your mind a bit about Rwanda). Reading these books, I found myself weeping at the horrors, admiring the bravery, hoping for the best, and always feeling entirely grateful I was living in peaceful Seattle. But—let me emphasize—they are all absolutely worth reading.

There are also seemingly innumerable stories of exploration and discovery, mostly to be found in dusty sections of libraries and used bookstores. There are books galore on colonial Africa (much of what is in them is now totally politically incorrect). And there are the novels, literary and otherwise, in which Africa plays an important role: Barbara Kingsolver's **The Poisonwood Bible**, for one; and **Green City in the Sun** by Barbara Wood (historical fiction set in Kenya) for another.

To make it simpler for readers (and myself), I've tried to list books under their specific settings, while including the general Africa titles, or those that cover more than one country, in this section.

Basil Davidson was one of the first white writers to suggest that Africa had a history and culture (amazingly enough, this came as shocking news to many people). He wrote a ton of books and they're somewhat dated, but **The Lost Cities of Africa** and **The Search for Africa: History, Culture, Politics** together will give you a good grounding in African history.

Although I would count Paul Theroux's **The Great Railway Bazaar** as one of my all-time favorite books, I found that the later accounts of his travels expressed such a dyspeptic view of the people he met and the places he was visiting that I was disinclined to go on reading them. I hadn't picked up another book of his (fiction or nonfiction) after the somewhat ironically titled **The Happy Isles of Oceania**, published in 1992, until a trusted book-recommending friend suggested **Dark Star Safari: Overland from Cairo to Cape Town**. In it, I discovered a hodgepodge of history, anecdotes, opinions, and description. I was immediately hooked by how Theroux begins his tale:

> All news out of Africa is bad. It made me want to
> go there, though not for the horror, the hot spots,

There are few more fatiguing experiences than to mingle with the holiday-makers of the Jamaican North Shore, all older, fatter, richer, idler and more ugly than oneself. India is full of splendours that must be seen now or perhaps never, but can a man of fifty-five long endure a regime where wine is prohibited?

One of my favorite discoveries at a used bookstore where I was poking around for armchair travel reading was Peter Biddlecombe's **French Lessons in Africa: Travels with My Briefcase Through French Africa**. In often hilarious and sometimes merely very funny anecdotes, Biddlecombe brings Francophone Africa, from Benin to Zaire, alive for us. Although this was published in 1994, not much of what Biddlecombe observed then has changed—or at least not changed for the better. If you can forget that depressing aspect, reading this is a delight.

And for an excellent and useful selection of recent writing from Africa, take a look at **Gods and Soldiers: The Penguin Anthology of Contemporary African Writing**, edited by Rob Spillman. It's filled with authors both familiar (like Chinua Achebe) and unfamiliar to most of us (like Alain Mabanckou—or at least he was to me, before I read his selection).

ALBANIA

Should you find yourself planning an excursion to Albania, the perfect accompaniment to the trip is Dorothy Gilman's **The Unexpected Mrs. Pollifax**, the first of a series (each novel is set in a different country). Widowed and bored with her life as a suburban woman-of-a-certain-age, she goes to the CIA head-quarters and volunteers to become a spy. Through a series of comic mishaps and misunderstandings, she's sent to Albania to locate the whereabouts of an agent who has disappeared. In the process, you learn (painlessly) about the history, politics, and geography of a country that is typically regarded as a cipher to many people.

The major (and very prolific) Albanian writer—a poet and novelist—is Ismail Kadare, who won the Man Booker International Award in 2005, and some day, I believe, he'll win the Nobel Prize for literature. Try **The Siege** (a historical novel about the fifteenth-century war with the Turks) or **Chronicle in Stone** (World War II in the life of a small boy and his vividly described town). The latter is one of those books that make you wish you could go back in time to spend a few moments in the place Kadare is describing.

When I first saw the title—**Edward Lear in Albania**—I was excited to find that one of my favorite nonsense poets (author of "The Owl and the Pussycat," etc.) had also traveled the wide world o'er. Then I looked more closely and read the subtitle: *Journals of a Landscape Painter in the Balkans*. It took me a minute to realize that there must have been two Edward Lears, and this was the one I was unfamiliar with. So of course I had to learn all about him and the trip he took through Albania and Macedonia in 1848, with paintbrush in hand. Lear's keen eye for subjects translated into a sharp interest in his surroundings, both the people he met and the places he visited. This book, edited by Bejtullah Destani and Robert Elsie, is a lovely piece of book art and a captivating read.

ALL SET FOR ALASKA

I emailed my pal Dana Stabenow, fabulous mystery writer and Alaska native, for suggestions of good books about Alaska. Her list—as only befits the kind of person she is—is eclectic and enticing. I've also added a few of my own suggestions at the end. Dana's comments are in quotation marks, while mine are not.

Dana's choices:

Confederate Raider in the North Pacific by Murray Morgan: "The last shot fired in the Civil War? It was fired in the Aleutians, by the CSS *Shenandoah*, on a mission to attack the Yankee whaling ships in an attempt to disrupt the North's economy. For rebels, these guys are almost too good to be true—no man is murdered, no woman is outraged, and I don't think they lose a single crewmember. Wonderfully engaging and well-written tale."

Good Time Girls of the Alaska-Yukon Gold Rush by Lael Morgan: "A story of the girls who came north with the rest of the stampeders to mine the miners in saloons, dance halls, and hook shops from Dawson to Nome to Cordova. Many of them came because they could only make a dollar a day as a farm hand Outside. A you-are-there picture of a place and time."

The Last Light Breaking by Nick Jans: "The story of a white man in an Inupiaq world. Beautifully written eyewitness account of a hunter-gatherer culture being rear-ended by the modern world."

The Thousand-Mile War by Brian Garfield: "This is a page-turning account of World War II as it was fought in the Aleutians. Reads like a Tom Clancy novel."

Two Old Women by Velma Wallis: "An old Athabascan tale re-imagined by a modern Athabascan writer. Very controversial in the Alaska Native community."

The book that was next on her list of "to reads"? **Fifty Miles from Tomorrow** by William L. Iggiagruk Hensley: "Inupiaq kid from Kotzebue grows up to shepherd the Alaska Native Claims Settlement Act through Congress, leading to the empowerment of Alaska's Native peoples." (You can watch my interview with Stabenow at www.seattlechannel.org/videos/video.asp?ID=3030905.)

And here are a few more Alaska titles to add to your growing pile of books:

If you'd like a sense of Alaska thirty or more years ago, you won't want to miss John McPhee's classic **Coming Into the Country**.

In **Tide, Feather, Snow: A Life in Alaska**, Miranda Weiss describes her experiences moving to Homer, Alaska, from her New Jersey home.

Robert Specht and Anne Purdy's **Tisha: The Wonderful True Love Story of a Young Teacher in the Alaska Wilderness** takes place in Chicken, Alaska. Schoolteacher Anne Hobbs leaves "civilization" to work in the Alaska bush. It's a good companion read to Benedict and Nancy Freedman's classic novel, **Mrs. Mike**. Although set in the Canadian wilderness and not Alaska, it shares with **Tisha** much of the same feel.

Working on the Edge by Spike Walker is a you-are-there account of king crab fishing.

One Man's Wilderness: An Alaskan Odyssey by Sam Keith (from the journals and photographs of naturalist Richard Proenneke) is the story of how, in the late 1960s, Proenneke decided to build

AMERICAN GIRLS

Americans abroad has always been a popular theme with novelists, and the novels that are particularly appealing feature young women who, despite the fact that they're totally out of their league, appear to thrive. Or not. Here are some of my favorites.

Of course, all novels about female Americans abroad owe a debt to Henry James and his singular creation, Isabel Archer, the heroine of **The Portrait of a Lady**. (Many of them also owe at least a little something to Truman Capote's greatest invention, Holly Golightly, heroine and heartbreaker of **Breakfast at Tiffany's**, but that's not my subject here.)

Elaine Dundy's **The Dud Avocado**, a fizzy cocktail of a novel, was originally published in 1958 (the same year as Capote's novel, in fact). It chronicles life among American expatriates in Paris in the 1950s as seen through the eyes of twenty-one-year-old Sally Jay Gorce, who arrives wide-eyed and innocent from Missouri, eager to experience all that Paris has to offer. The story is more than a little autobiographical, and you can't help but try to identify the expats Dundy describes. But don't trust me on the charms of this recently re-issued novel: no less a literary critic than Groucho Marx declared when it first appeared that "I had to tell someone how much I enjoyed *The Dud Avocado*. It made me laugh, scream, and guffaw (which, incidentally, is a great name for a law firm)."

Dundy also wrote about the swinging London of the early 1960s in **The Old Man and Me**. The heroine—now older, wiser, and much more cunning (not to say bitter) than Sally Jay Gorce—is

Honey Flood. It's not as much pure fun to read, but is still a perfect evocation of a time and place long past.

England is also the setting of **Do Try to Speak as We Do** by Marjorie Leet Ford (some editions were called **The Diary of an American Au Pair**). This humorous diary of a young woman working for an upper-class family is filled with the Brits' reactions to Americans living in England, and the everlasting confusion and embarrassment Americans experience with Briticisms and cultural etiquette.

Two lighthearted fictional accounts of Americans in Paris can be found in Diane Johnson's **Le Divorce** and **Le Mariage**.

Cornelia Otis Skinner's **Our Hearts Were Young and Gay** is one of my favorite cozy reads—it's the true story of the European adventures of Skinner and her good friend Emily Kimbrough (check the index of *Book Lust To Go* for books by Kimbrough—they're equally entertaining). Skinner and Kimbrough's experiences will have you chuckling for hours.

AN ANGLOPHILE'S LITERARY PILGRIMAGE

Setting off on a voyage usually requires a map and, if you're Great Britain–bound, none could be better than **A Literary Atlas and Gazetteer of the British Isles** by Michael

Hardwick and Alan G. Hodgkiss. Hodgkiss, a cartographer, and Hardwick, a writer, take readers on a detailed journey through the large and small literary landmarks of Great Britain with maps, photos, bibliographies, and biographies. By following their directions readers can find all kinds of wonders. For example, in Nuneaton there is a statue of George Eliot in the middle of a busy square, and in the nearby museum are Eliot's writing desk and a range of her dresses. The landscape of Nuneaton is vividly described in Eliot's novels (most particularly **The Mill on the Floss** and **Adam Bede**) and current-day visitors to Nuneaton can still see the wooded walks and "capricious hedgerows" of Eliot's world.

Taking a turn to the north, readers can follow the steep and winding hills to the Brontë Parsonage. If you have ever wondered how Emily Brontë dreamed her moody landscapes and vast expanses of heath and doom, you only have to gaze upon the lichen-darkened tombstones she saw out her window every day, and beyond them to the endless land that beckons with its boggy ground. It's a grand thing to find a book whose tone so well matches its landscape, but **Wuthering Heights** exceeds even this high mark, inhabiting the land to the point that the narrative is every rock and crag, as well as every letter and line.

Much lighter in view and tone is the home of Jane Austen in Chawton. In the well-tended seventeenth-century red brick house, Austen wrote **Mansfield Park**, **Emma**, and **Persuasion**, and revised for publication **Pride and Prejudice**, **Sense and Sensibility**, and **Northanger Abbey**. The stress on family and houses, village life and open landscapes for walking, are all seen at Chawton, only fifty miles from London, but located in a small village. Austen spent eight years at Chawton, and it gave her space and a sense of being settled, both of which appear as themes in her novels. Visitors can experience the same space and ease Austen felt from her well-tended garden, tiny writing desk, and large decorative windows with their view of the village streets.

As glorious as the villages and heaths of England are, it is London that serves as the literary heartbeat of the Isles. Less than an hour from Austen's home sits the city of Dickens and Shakespeare—as well as Virginia Woolf. Woolf loved walking in London, and set herself and her characters off on long rambles through the city. There is a great deal of Woolf's London left to see in the streets, squares, and parks. The urban landscape of London, marked by the chiming of Big Ben, makes for a great walk for fans of **Mrs. Dalloway**. Begin at Westminster and ramble up Victoria Street to cross through St. James's Park, out to Piccadilly, and then up Bond Street to Oxford Street. As you do, think about the rumble of omnibuses and busy shop fronts, and of Septimus enduring his hallucinations in Regent's Park.

After taking in the sweeping order of Regent's Park, wander back down to Westminster Abbey, enter its cool, dark corridors, and head to the South Transept and Poet's Corner. Here you'll find a hodge-podge of sculpture, tablets, and signs, all forming a mosaic in honor of the literary greats of England. Chaucer, Browning, Dickens, Hardy, and Tennyson are actually buried here, but memorials exist for Byron, Shakespeare, Austen, Blake, the Brontës, George Eliot, and dozens of others as well. It's amazing to stand in the recalled company of so many voices and quite enough to send you scurrying to Stratford or Tintagel, with Hodgkiss and Hardwick as your irreplaceable guides.

seemingly doomed nation ever since. Here are some books I can highly recommend:

Winner of the National Book Award in 1976, **Passage to Ararat** by Michael J. Arlen is an exploration of his own cultural heritage and his family's former homeland.

Other books that will give you a good sense of the country include Peter Balakian's **Black Dog of Fate: A Memoir**; Joan London's novel **Gilgamesh**, set just as World War II was beginning; Micheline Aharonian Marcom's tragic novel **Three Apples Fell from Heaven**; and Vartan Gregorian's memoir **The Road to Home: My Life and Times**.

AUSTRALIA, THE LAND OF OZ

I've been lucky enough to spend some time (with family, librarians, and readers) in Australia. It's one of my favorite places not only to visit but also to read about. Some of my top picks follow.

The Literature of Australia: An Anthology has an informative introduction by one of the country's best novelists, Thomas Keneally. It's a collection filled with excerpts from novels and works of nonfiction, as well as poetry. It also includes writings of the Aboriginal peoples (which sets it apart from many earlier collections). Because it's arranged chronologically, I think you'll find that it's a good place to experience the development and range of Australian literature and get a sense of who you want to read next.

Nonfiction

Once there were two families, one Australian, one American: each family had a mother, a father who worked for his country's foreign service, and two little girls. The older two girls were the same age, while the younger two—one of them Jane Alison, the author of **The Sisters Antipodes**, whose memoir this is—shared the same birthday, although Jenny was a year older. Jane describes the events that followed when the adults got divorced in order to exchange spouses: Jane was four, and her older sister, Patricia, was seven. In less than a year, it was all over: two divorces, two remarriages, new fathers, and a new life. Although this is less about Australia than probably warrants including it here, I couldn't resist because I enjoyed it so much.

Before she became a reporter and best-selling and award-winning novelist, Geraldine Brooks was a child growing up in Sydney. Her memoir of those years—which gives a good indication of the kind of adult she became—is **Foreign Correspondence**. My discussion with Brooks can be found at: www.seattlechannel.org/videos/video.asp?ID=3030807.

Peter Carey's **30 Days in Sydney: A Wildly Distorted Account** is delightfully idiosyncratic. (But don't miss his **True History of the Kelly Gang**—you can go to the State Library of Victoria and see Kelly's unusual set of armor, as well as Carey's manuscript for the novel.)

Australian Tim Flannery is an incredibly prolific writer and editor. Two of his books that I've most enjoyed and that are especially applicable here are **Chasing Kangaroos: A Continent, a Scientist,** and a Search for the World's Most Extraordinary Creature and **The Explorers: Stories of Discovery and Adventure from the Australian Frontier**. Just looking at the cover of the former gives you a sense of the book: A kangaroo is reclining under a bright blue sky and hot Australian sun, his (or her) ears perked up, a bird perched on one flank, staring out at you from beneath hooded eyes, looking for all the world like a creature out of *Alice in Wonderland*. You can almost imagine her (or him) saying, "Welcome to my strange and wonderful world. Prepare to be amazed." Not to accept that invitation is to miss out on one of the most delightfully informative books I've read lately. The latter book, edited by Flannery, is a collection of sixty-seven entries by men who were "flies on the wall" during a meaningful moment in Australian history. The entries range from 1606, when the first European saw the continent, right up to the twentieth century.

Greater Nowheres: Wanderings Across the Outback is by two American writers and outdoorsmen. Dave Finkelstein and Jack London (not the same man who wrote *The Call of the Wild*) set out to find a man-eating crocodile known as the "deadly salty" and along the way encounter enough unusual sights, sounds, and experiences to make this book so enjoyable.

Other fabulous nonfiction about the country includes **The Dig Tree: The Extraordinary Story of the Ill-Fated Burke and Wills 1860 Expedition** by Sarah Murgatroyd; **Daisy Bates in the Desert: A Woman's Life Among the Aborigines** by Julia Blackburn; **The Last Explorer: Hubert Wilkins: Australia's Unknown Hero** by Simon Nasht, which is the story of a man who wore many hats: reporter, photographer, scientist, and spy; and

A. B. Facey's **A Fortunate Life**, which is a memoir covering most of the twentieth century, set in small settlements in the outback. Despite Facey's horribly difficult childhood, this remarkable work has no trace of irony at all, and the title must be taken quite literally. It makes for a moving and powerful book. Two other excellent memoirs are **In Sunshine or in Shadow**, Martin Flanagan's moving account of trying to understand Tasmania's past—and that of five generations of his own family—and Robyn Davidson's **Tracks**, her story of walking across Australia's desert accompanied by four camels in the 1970s.

Fiction

The sense of the city I got from **The Unknown Terrorist** (grungy and scary) seemed far removed from the Sydney I visited (and loved) in 2006 and 2007. But Richard Flanagan has written an amazing, if uncomfortable, novel (as all of his are) that's totally in tune with today's world of terrorism and paranoia. Flanagan, born in Tasmania, can't seem to write a bad sentence; I always look forward to reading his books and seeing what he's up to next.

When I was in Australia, a fellow librarian and good friend suggested that I might like Peter Temple's **The Broken Shore**, an emotionally powerful and complex thriller that takes place outside Melbourne. Through his main character, homicide detective Joe Cashin, Temple raises important issues about the seemingly endemic prejudice against the aboriginal peoples. Written in the style of Richard Price, Dennis Lehane, and George Pelecanos, Temple brings out the soul of Australia's past and present.

And more fiction that absolutely shouldn't be missed includes all of Kate Grenville's novels, especially **The Secret River** and **The Lieutenant**; anything by Helen Garner, such as **The Children's Bach** (now rather old and somewhat hard to get a copy of) and **Monkey Grip**; the mysteries of Adrian Hyland, featuring a half-aboriginal amateur detective named Emily Tempest and set in the Australian outback—the first is **Moonlight Downs** and the second is **Gunshot Road**; Frank Hardy's **Power Without Glory**, which caused a huge scandal when it was first (self-)published in 1950; and Elizabeth Jolley's **The Vera Wright Trilogy**, comprised of **My Father's Moon**, **Cabin Fever**, and **The Georges' Wife**.

AZ YOU LIKE IT

R ichard Shelton's **Going Back to Bisbee** was the first book I encountered that made me think I might find that the Arizona desert has as much beauty as the Pacific Northwest's forests and lakes. In the years since I first read his memoir, I've discovered other fine Arizona reads:

Natural history buffs won't want to miss any of the books by Craig Childs, wilderness and river guide, solitary wanderer, and obsessive desert lover. My favorite is **The Animal Dialogues: Uncommon Encounters in the Wild**, but since it's not strictly Arizona-centric, try **The Secret Knowledge of Water: Discovering the Essence of the American Desert** instead. (There seem to be different subtitles on different editions or printings of the book, so sometimes it reads *There Are Two Easy Ways to Die in the Desert: Thirst and Drowning*.)

Two enjoyable character-driven novels about trips down the Colorado River are **In the Heart of the Canyon** by Elisabeth Hyde and **Ambition** by Lisa Michaels. Hyde's novel tells of a group of strangers who come together for a multi-day raft trip that manages to change the lives of all the participants. There's an irresistible dog as well, which should please canine lovers. Michaels' novel is the story of newlyweds whose 1928 honeymoon trip on the Colorado has unexpected consequences.

John Vernon's **The Last Canyon**, a fascinating biographical novel about John Wesley Powell, would make a good reading companion to Edward Dolnick's **Down the Great Unknown: John Wesley Powell's 1869 Journey of Discovery and Tragedy Through the Grand Canyon**. Each is eminently readable and describes, in very different ways, Powell and his crew's great, grand, and dangerous adventure.

There are many good reads, both fiction and nonfiction, about an important but bleak subject: the hazards of illegally crossing the Arizona-Mexico border. Two of the best novels I've discovered are Philip Caputo's **Crossers** and **Into the Beautiful North** by Luis Alberto Urrea. (Urrea is also the author of **The Devil's Highway**, a true story of illegal immigrants trying to survive the brutalities of sun, thirst, and the U.S. Border Patrol in the part of the Arizona desert known as "the devil's highway.") All three are good choices for book groups.

Mysteries set in Arizona are plentiful. They include Ross Mac-Donald's **The Blue Hammer** (you can never go wrong with a Lew Archer thriller, no matter where they're set); Louise Ure's **Liars Anonymous,** featuring Jessie Dancing, who works for an emergency road service company in Phoenix; and **New River Blues** by Elizabeth Gunn, whose main character, Sarah Burke, is a detective with the Tucson Police Department.

If you're up for a bit of historical fantasy, try Emma Bull's most wonderful **Territory**—a re-imagining of the events leading up to the famous shootout at the O.K. Corral in Tombstone, Arizona, in 1881. Wyatt Earp, Doc Holliday, and others all make appearances. About Doc Holliday, Bull writes, " . . . no amount of wanting would make Doc an upstanding member of the community. He was a fine dentist—he just wasn't a fine person. And he was so good at being bad that it seemed like a genuine gift. One ought not to waste one's gifts." I was especially intrigued by the way Bull made use of the belief so prevalent among nineteenth-century men and women— that one can go west and reinvent him- or herself, which is a major theme of the novel. As one character explains to another, "You're whoever you say you are, Millie. That's the point of coming west."

THE BALTIC STATES

The history of the Baltic States—Lithuania, Latvia, and Estonia—is marked with disasters. It was annexed (and occupied) first by the Soviet Union (in 1939), then by Germany (1941–1944), and then again by the Soviet Union (1944–1991). In fact, when I was in Estonia a few years ago, various people would remind me that for them, World War II didn't end until the last Soviet soldier left the country in 1994.

As a result, much of the writing from these three countries is not going to be particularly upbeat, and as readers we're hampered by the fact that most books have never been translated into English. I kept asking my new Estonian friends what books I should read to help me understand their country, and the Baltic world in general, but not only are books quite expensive, most of what's in the bookstores in Tallinn (the capital of Estonia) were translations of British and American best sellers. (Terry Pratchett and Jayne Ann Krentz were *very* popular on both library and bookstore shelves.)

Here are some worthy books that I discovered after my all-too-short trip there had ended.

Mati Unt's experimental novel **Brecht at Night** is definitely not for those who like conventional narratives, but if you're up for something a bit different, here's the book for you. I loved the weirdness of it.

Jaan Kross's **The Conspiracy and Other Stories, Treading Air**, and **The Czar's Madman** all deal with how fate (for which, I think, one can read "history") has in one way or another denied the characters their well-earned futures.

Sofi Oksanen is Finnish-Estonian, and she sets her novel **Purge** in Estonia; the book (the first of her writing to appear in English) ranges back and forth in time over the twentieth century and gives us—along with a good story—a solid grounding in the grueling history of Estonia.

Life under the Nazi regime and then as a refugee in a "displaced person's camp" is faithfully described in **The Rings of My Tree:**

A Latvian Woman's Journey by Jane E. Cunningham. It's the story of her friend Mirdza's experiences before, during, and after World War II.

And these: **Red Weather** by Pauls Toutonghi, about a fifteen-year-old who moves with his family from Latvia to Milwaukee at the end of the Cold War; Henning Mankell sends his investigator Kurt Wallender from Sweden to Latvia in **The Dogs of Riga**; **There Once Was a World: A 900-Year Chronicle of the Shtetl of Eishyshok** by Yaffa Eliach; **The Fire Escape Is Locked for Your Safety: On the Road in the Former Soviet Union** by Molly J. Baier; **The Issa Valley** by Czeslaw Milosz; Mark Kurzem's **The Mascot: Unraveling the Mystery of My Jewish Father's Nazi Boyhood**; Antony Sher's **Middlepost**; **Ticket to Latvia: A Journey from Berlin to the Baltic** by Marcus Tanner; and Hillel Levine's **In Search of Sugihara: The Elusive Japanese Diplomat Who Risked His Life to Rescue 10,000 Jews from the Holocaust** (in Lithuania).

BALTIMORE

Quite honestly, I can't imagine a visit to Baltimore—either really going there or visiting from the comfort of my couch—without first watching the television program *The Wire*, co-created by David Simon. Simon is also the co-author (with Edward Burns) of the best nonfiction book about Baltimore that I've ever read—**The Corner: A Year in the Life of an Inner-City Neighborhood** (which was the basis for *The Wire*). Simon also wrote **Homicide: A Year on the Killing Streets**, also set in Baltimore (and became another top-notch television show). I'd also definitely rent Barry Levinson's film *Diner* and watch that for another, less bleak, view of the city.

When it comes to fiction, the majority of Anne Tyler's novels are set in Baltimore—in fact, in a particular part of Baltimore: Roland Park—but setting isn't Tyler's thing (that would be character), so you don't get much sense of the city. Of course, any time you have the opportunity to read an Anne Tyler novel (try **Searching for Caleb**) you should probably do so!

You'll get a better taste of Baltimore life by reading the mystery series by Laura Lippman (all featuring ex–*Baltimore Sun* reporter, now private eye Tess Monaghan), in which the city functions as almost another character. I'm not convinced you need to read them in order, although if you're so inclined, the first is **Baltimore Blues**. One of my favorites is **In a Strange City**, in which Edgar Allan Poe, whose hometown is Baltimore and who is buried there, features prominently in the plot.

Other good Baltimore-set reading includes:

Ta-Nehisi Coates's **The Beautiful Struggle: A Father, Two Sons, and an Unlikely Road to Manhood** depicts the author's life growing up on the tough streets of Baltimore. Who could have predicted he would become a well-known writer and blogger?

The first time I saw Baltimore's rebuilt Inner Harbor area, with its new restaurants and a fabulous aquarium, I couldn't help remembering the glory years of Baltimore's football team, the Colts. (What can I say? For many years I was a die-hard football fan.) This was during the 1950s and '60s, two decades and more before the night of infamy—March 29, 1984—when owner Robert Irsay snuck the team out of Baltimore to its new home in Indianapolis. And that reminded me that if you have any interest in football at all, don't miss Mark Bowden's superb history, **The Best Game Ever: Giants vs. Colts, 1958, and the Birth of the Modern NFL**. You'll feel as though you were actually at the National Football League championship game, down on the field with Johnny Unitas, receiver Raymond Berry, and the other Colts, playing on a frigid day in Yankee Stadium. Even though the book (and the game itself) wasn't set in Baltimore, it really fits into this section.

BERLIN

I spent not nearly enough time in Berlin last year, but I realized almost immediately that for any history buff, Berlin is the place to go—you're surrounded by remnants of the past, from the charming walk/stop traffic signals in the former East Berlin and the references to Checkpoint Charlie, to the chillingly brilliant Memorial to the Murdered Jews of Europe and the Daniel Libeskind–designed Jewish Museum. Here are some books you won't want to miss reading, either before you go or after you return home.

After wandering around the Alexanderplatz section of the city in the rain and cold on my visit there, I was moved to track down a copy of Alfred Döblin's 1929 masterpiece **Berlin Alexanderplatz: The Story of Franz Biberkopf**. What a pleasure it was to read.

What I Saw: Reports from Berlin 1920–1933 is a collection of Joseph Roth's newspaper columns; his incisive vision of the present and the future of Berlin (and Germany) is presented through his immaculate prose. (And Roth's novels and short stories are spectacular, particularly **The Radetzky March**.)

Zoo Station: Adventures in East and West Berlin by Ian Walker, published in 1988, gives a vivid picture of the fractured city in the period leading up to the fall of the Berlin Wall.

There are many novels set during the period of the Cold War and the divided city, but two especially remarkable ones are Ian McEwan's **The Innocent** (written before he became a household name) and John le Carré's **The Spy Who Came in from the Cold**.

The Australian writer and lawyer Anna Funder collected the stories of many East Berliners living during the Cold War. Their Orwellian tales are collected in **Stasiland: Stories from Behind the Berlin Wall**.

You can't get a better sense of Berlin between the wars than by reading Otto Friedrich's **Before the Deluge: A Portrait of Berlin in the 1920s**. It would be so interesting to use this as a guidebook to present-day Berlin.

Three mysteries that noir fans will likely adore are Philip Kerr's **March Violets**, **The Pale Criminal**, and **A German Requiem**, set from the early 1930s to 1947 and all featuring detective Bernie Günter.

But perhaps my favorite book about Berlin, set about a decade before World War II, when people in the know began to foresee what was coming, is Christopher Isherwood's **The Berlin Stories**, consisting of **The Last of Mr. Norris** and **Goodbye to Berlin**. It became, of course, the hit play *Cabaret*.

BORNEO AND SARAWAK

There aren't a huge number of books about Borneo and Sarawak to recommend to would-be travelers, and the area does have a somewhat grisly reputation as being the home of all those head-hunting Dayaks, but for folks willing to take on the adventure of it all, try these wildly divergent books, all set in Borneo.

Fair warning: Andro Linklater's **Wild People: Travels with Borneo's Head-Hunters** is not for the squeamish, but if you read the disturbing sections really quickly and linger over the others, you'll get a good picture of the region.

Stranger in the Forest: On Foot Across Borneo by Eric Hansen could just as easily have gone in the section called "It Seemed Like a Good Idea at the Time"—I'm not sure anyone would really want to follow in Hansen's footsteps, but it certainly makes for an unforgettable book.

Kalimantaan by C. S. Godshalk supposedly has legions of devoted readers—yet I rarely meet anyone with whom I can discuss it. *Kalimantaan* is a big biographical novel about a young man named Gideon Barr who makes his way to Borneo in 1838, when it was just a little-known island in the South China Sea. It's the kind of book that has a bit of everything and encompasses almost every issue the Victorians were dealing with: colonialism, a woman's role in society, and racial issues.

When people mention Judith Heimann's **The Airmen and the Headhunters: A True Story of Lost Soldiers, Heroic Tribesmen, and the Unlikeliest Rescue of World War II** to me, they always use terms like "reads like a novel" or "page-turning." They're right. Not only is this is a treat for history buffs, it's also a natural for fans of anthropology-for-the-layman books. And the best part is that what could have been an awfully depressing event ends happily.

Among his variety of occupations, Tom Harrisson was one of the first anthropologists who showed a deep respect in his writing for the civilization of the cannibalistic cultures he studied in the New Hebrides. He wrote about his experience in **Savage Civilisation**, published in 1937 and long out of print. But Judith Heimann's biography—**The Most Offending Soul Alive: Tom Harrisson and His Remarkable Life**—brings him to vivid life.

Mountain climbing in Borneo? Yes indeed, as described most entertainingly in Sam Lightner's **All Elevations Unknown: An Adventure in the Heart of Borneo**. Lightner and a few friends traveled to Borneo as a result of reading **World Within**, Harrisson's memoir of his adventures in the country during World War II.

Biruté Galdikas is one of the three women primate researchers who worked with Dr. Louis Leakey. She's probably much less well known than either Jane Goodall (who studies chimpanzees) or Dian Fossey (who studied gorillas). Galdikas's area of expertise is the orangutan, and she's based in Borneo. Despite the fact that I rarely remember how to properly pronounce the word orangutan—I always somehow put an extra "g" at the end of it—I love reading about Galdikas's studies of them in their natural habitat. I guarantee that after you read her memoir **Reflections of Eden: My Years with the Orangutans of Borneo**, you'll never look at an orangutan in a zoo the same way again.

Agnes Newton Keith's moving **Three Came Home** is the story of what she, her husband, and their young son experienced in a Japanese internment camp in Borneo during World War II. It was first published in 1946, when the events of their incarceration were still seared into their minds. I still treasure my copy of Keith's book; I bought it way back in the early 1960s. I especially appreciate the relatively even-handed way she describes their Japanese guards and commanders.

To me, one of the most interesting facts about Sarawak, one of the states on the island of Borneo, is how closely connected its creation was to Sir James Brooke, who became known as the Rajah of Sarawak in 1842. (The painting of him in London's National Portrait Gallery by Sir Francis Grant portrays him as both charismatic and devastatingly handsome.) There aren't any great current biographies about him (and it would be wildly unadmirable to admire him), but if you're intrigued, try Emily Hahn's **James Brooke of Sarawak: A Biography of Sir James Brooke**.

BOSTON: BEANS, BIRD, AND THE RED SOX

For a contemporary view of Boston, try **The Good City**, edited by Emily Hiestand and Ande Zellman, which includes both descriptive and personal essays on everything Boston from the Isabella Stewart Gardner Museum to various sports teams, all written by a variety of authors. This should probably be required reading for anyone heading to Beantown.

Boston appears to be an incredibly felonious city—particularly if you count the number of detectives and private eyes who operate out of it.

Try Robert B. Parker's Spenser series (one of the best is **The Judas Goat**, which is set relatively early in both Parker's and Spenser's careers).

For personal reasons (which you'll totally understand when you read the novel), my favorite of Linda Barnes's Carlotta Carlyle series remains **Cold Case**. (You can watch my interview with Barnes at www.seattlechannel.org/videos/video.asp?ID=3030607.)

I find Tess Gerritsen's Jane Rizzoli series—she's a Boston homicide detective—to be a bit edgy and not for the faint of heart. If you're up for it, start with the first one, **The Surgeon**.

Dennis Lehane's novels about private investigators Patrick Kenzie and Angela Gennaro provide many enjoyable hours of reading. I'd read them in order, beginning with the first, and still one of the best, **Prayers for Rain**.

And because sports are such a big part of the Boston zeitgeist, baseball fans shouldn't miss **Game Six: Cincinnati, Boston, and the 1975 World Series: The Triumph of America's Pastime** by Mark Frost, and basketball fanatics will thoroughly enjoy Michael Connelly's **Rebound!: Basketball, Busing, Larry Bird, and the Rebirth of Boston**.

The Last Night at the Ritz by Elizabeth Savage is in my top five for all-time favorite novels. Set partially in Boston, it's one of those titles that I keep wishing someone would reissue in a lovely trade paperback edition so I can replace the falling-apart old copy I picked up at some thrift store years ago.

BOTSWANA

If Alexander McCall Smith didn't exist, I suspect that the Botswana Tourist Bureau (assuming there is one) would have to invent him.

It's Smith's collection of tales featuring Precious Ramotswe, who is, as she says, "blessed with girth rather than height," that brought this African country (bigger than California and smaller than Texas, located between Zimbabwe and South Africa) to readers looking for interesting characters and a setting that functions as much as a character as any of the other, two-legged sort. From **The No. 1 Ladies' Detective Agency**, **Tears of the Giraffe**, and on through **Tea Time for the Traditionally Built**, which is my favorite title, Smith offers hours of pleasure reading.

After living for many years in New Zealand, Robyn Scott's small-plane-flying physician father and ever-up-for-an-adventure mother returned to their Botswana home in 1987. In **Twenty Chickens for a Saddle: The Story of an African Childhood**, Scott describes what life was like in a deserted mining town far from any city of significant size.

A Carrion Death by Michael Stanley is the first mystery featuring a Botswanan policeman named David Bengu, whose fellow cops have nicknamed him "Kubu," which is Setswanan (a Botswanan dialect) for hippopotamus, thus successfully describing his appearance. This series (as I write this, there are only two—the other is **The Second Death of Goodluck Tinubu**) is *much* grittier and faster-paced than Smith's novels. They're perfect to take on the plane as you're heading off on safari (or just flying from Cleveland to Seattle, for that matter).

Whatever You Do, Don't Run: True Tales of a Botswana Safari Guide by Peter Allison is an awfully funny collection of essays about trying to herd human animals to safe viewing of herds of nonhuman animals. If this doesn't make you want to sign up immediately for a trek with the Australian-by-birth Allison, I don't know what will.

Bessie Head, born in South Africa of a white mother and black father (at a time when that was not only frowned upon, but patently illegal), moved to Botswana in 1964. One of her best-known novels is **When Rain Clouds Gather**. One librarian described it to me this way: "It's about a community of exiles in Botswana as they try both to modernize (read, westernize) their way of farming while simultaneously holding on to their heritage."

BRAZIL

In 1978, after he's forced—due to failing health—to abandon his farm in Ecuador, Moritz Thomsen takes a journey through Brazil, making stops in Rio, Bahia, Recife, Natal, and Fortaleza, and ending with a longish sojourn on the Amazon River. I found his memoir of this trip, **The Saddest Pleasure: A Journey on Two Rivers**, to be utterly enthralling. (Graham Greene once described travel as "the saddest pleasure.") Originally published in

1990 and now, alas, long out of print, it is much more than the story of Thomsen's trip: indeed, the trip becomes a metaphor for his life. The book is filled with quotable lines: "I have become," he mourns, "that person who is of no interest to anyone and about whom no one will have the slightest curiosity. I have become to all intents and purposes invisible." On his flight to Brazil he changes planes in Colombia, and, watching the sun set there, says, "For a few moments corrupt, chaotic Colombia shines as magically beautiful as paradise." And he has a great comment about the whole tour-ist experience: "Famous sites seen by too many eyes are robbed little by little of their power to excite or dazzle; each pair of eyes has taken something away. Public things are diminished by lying helpless under the public gaze." And this: "There is no way to live with the illusion of being made happy by the things that one owns, especially in a country like Ecuador where a comparative handful of people own everything, without developing an armor of blind-ness that makes one not only insensitive but contemptuous of the overwhelming poverty through which one moves."

I encountered Thomsen's memoir right after I read Paul Theroux's **Dark Star Safari**, and was interested to find that Theroux wrote the introduction to Thomsen's book, and, on their respective trips, both men read and reread the fiction of Joseph Conrad.

As Thomsen says in his memoir, Brazilian literature is dominated by Jorge Amado (**Gabriela, Clove, and Cinnamon** and **Dona Flor and Her Two Husbands** are the best known) but Eduardo Galeano's Memory of Fire trilogy (made up of **Genesis, Faces and Masks**, and **Century of the Wind**) is a useful introduction to South American history and culture.

And mystery fans can rejoice in reading Luiz Alfredo Garcia-Roza's complex novels featuring Inspector Espinosa. Try **Blackout** or **Alone in the Crowd**.

If you enjoy cerebral puzzlers, try Luis Fernando Verissimo's **Borges and the Eternal Orangutans**, a short and brilliant novel about a murder that occurs at a convention of Edgar Allan Poe scholars in Buenos Aires. Jorge Luis Borges is a central character, which should give you a hint of what you're in for here. I simply loved it.

BURMESE DAYS

This is the last section I wrote for *Book Lust To Go*, because it wasn't until six weeks after the manuscript was done that I realized I had forgotten to include some wonderful books about the country. But I was torn about what to call the section. Any title would be a political statement. In the end, I went with the title above, rather than something like, for example, "Myanmar Musings."

Burmese Days is George Orwell's more-than-somewhat autobiographical novel of a British ex-pat living in a fictional district in Burma in the 1920s, when the end of Empire was foreseen by smart Englishmen. Orwell worked for the Indian Imperial Police force for five years, beginning in 1922. (At that time Burma was considered a part of India.)

When I discovered Emma Larkin's fascinating **Finding George Orwell in Burma**, I was taken (as many have been, before me) by her description of Orwell's more famous novels being a metaphor for most of twentieth-century Burmese history. To some Burmese, she tells us, Orwell is known as "the prophet." Larkin goes on to say:

> In Burma there is a joke that Orwell wrote not just one novel about the country, but three: a trilogy comprised of *Burmese Days*, *Animal Farm*, and *1984*.

The book is a combination of biography and armchair travel, as Larkin visits all the places where Orwell lived and worked. I found it totally riveting and immensely well written.

"Emma Larkin" is a pseudonym for an Asian-born, Burmese-speaking American journalist; and try as I might, I haven't been able to uncover more about her (or him). Her newest book is **Everything Is Broken: A Tale of Catastrophe in Burma**, about the devastation wreaked by cyclone Nargis in 2008 in the southwestern part of a country that was already politically devastated. If you've never heard about Nargis, don't fault your news-reading skills: the 100,000 or so deaths and associated destruction were both under-reported and suppressed by the Burmese government.

Mac McClelland's **For Us Surrender Is Out of the Question: A Story from Burma's Never-Ending War** is a memoir of the author's time spent working in Burma with a group fighting the country's dictatorship. Hard-edged and gripping, it's journalism at its best.

Other required (by me, at least) nonfiction reading includes Justin Wintle's **Perfect Hostage: A Life of Aung San Suu Kyi, Burma's Prisoner of Conscience**, a sympathetic portrait of the courageous 1991 Nobel Peace Prize winner who leads the resistance movement in Burma; **Letters from Burma**, a collection of Aung San Suu Kyi's own writings from the six years she spent under house arrest beginning in 1989; and Karen Connelly's **Burmese Lessons: A True Love Story**.

As for fiction, there are three novels too good to miss:

Karen Connelly's evocative **The Lizard Cage** was written before *Burmese Lessons*. It won the 2007 Orange Prize for New Writers and was one of the finalists for the Kiriyama Prize, which celebrates "literary voices of the Pacific Rim."

Amitav Ghosh's **The Glass Palace** is a sweeping work of historical fiction that begins in 1885 and ends in the present day. The events of the novel occur primarily in Burma, Malaya, and India. Ghosh writes about the evils of colonialism better than almost anyone else I've ever read (except maybe Paul Scott), but you never feel hit over the head with his message or overloaded by facts and details. His writing is superb and the characters are unforgettable.

The Piano Tuner by Daniel Mason takes place at the same time Ghosh's begins. It's the story of Edgar Drake, who is sent to Burma to repair a grand piano that's important to British colonial interests. Despite the event-filled plot, the main interest (and character) here is really the country itself. This is a great audio book for those of you who enjoy listening to well-read tales.

CAMBODIA

Cambodia suffered through years of political terror and repression—who can ever forget the phrase "the killing fields"? The books that follow certainly offer a testament to the human spirit, but do yourself a favor by taking a break with a funny or at least happy book in between reading these.

Stunning use of language and an almost elliptical writing style mark Kim Echlin's **The Disappeared**, the story of a young Canadian girl who falls in love with a Cambodian studying in Montreal. When the borders to his country are opened, Serey returns to Phnom Penh to try to locate his family. And more than a decade later, Anne Greves travels to Cambodia to find him. Echlin shows us that Anne's heartbreak and loss are not just due to the large political events in the world, but also to decisions made for other, more personal reasons.

Loung Ung's two memoirs, **First They Killed My Father: A Daughter of Cambodia Remembers** (life under Pol Pot's regime in the 1970s) and **Lucky Child: A Daughter of Cambodia Reunites with the Sister She Left Behind** (which tells of her return to Cambodia in 1995), are moving and honest; both read like novels, albeit sad ones.

When Broken Glass Floats: Growing Up Under the Khmer Rouge by Chanrithy Him offers another perspective on childhood during the reign of the Khmer Rouge. It's a heartbreaking and unforgettable read.

Dith Pran, the Cambodian photojournalist who was the subject of the film *The Killing Fields*, compiled **Children of Cambodia's Killing Fields: Memoirs by Survivors**.

Other nonfiction books set during that chilling period—from 1970 to 1975, when two million Cambodians were killed—that are almost certain to break your heart are **The Lost Executioner: A Journey to the Heart of the Killing Fields** by Nic Dunlop, a

Thailand-based, Irish photojournalist; François Bizot's **The Gate**; and **River of Time** by British journalist John Swain.

For a change of pace (and time period), try Norman Lewis's **A Dragon Apparent: Travels in Cambodia, Laos, and Vietnam**, originally published in England in 1951.

There isn't a lot of great fiction about Cambodia (or at least I haven't found much beyond Echlin's book) and what's out there is also not particularly aimed at making you feel better about the world, but two more of the best are Christopher J. Koch's **Highways to a War**, about a photojournalist who disappears in Cambodia in 1976, and John Del Vecchio's **For the Sake of All Living Things**, about a pair of siblings who choose different paths during the era of the Khmer Rouge.

CANADA, O CANADA

Because Miss Frances Whitehead, the children's librarian at the Parkman Branch library in Detroit, was Canadian, I think I was inoculated with a love of Canadian writers. If the jacket of a book says that the author is Canadian, I'll always pick it up and give it a try. Here are some you shouldn't miss.

If Bill Bryson is one of your favorite armchair travelers and storytellers, then I'm pretty certain you'll enjoy Will Ferguson's **Beauty Tips from Moose Jaw: Travels in Search of Canada**, because he writes about his native country with the same sort of affection (and occasional exasperation) as Bryson does. Ferguson describes not only the places he visits and the people he meets from Victoria to Newfoundland, but also includes tales of early explorers like Samuel Hearne, who, in 1770, walked from Prince of Wales Fort, on the shores of Hudson Bay, to the Arctic Ocean, and back again, a distance of some 5,600 kilometers, looking for the Northwest Passage and copper mines (and finding neither). Ferguson also describes his own experiences, such as watching polar bears from about as up close as anyone would want to get. Reading Ferguson's often laugh-aloud essays, I was reminded of just how vast and varied our neighbor to the north is.

Another enjoyable choice for those who enjoy off-the-beaten-track accounts is **Welcome Home: Travels in Smalltown Canada** by Stuart McLean. It includes vignettes from eight towns all over Canada, including Maple Creek, Saskatchewan; Dresden, Ontario; St.-Jean-de-Matha, Quebec; Sackville, New Brunswick; Oxwarren, Manitoba; Nakusp, British Columbia; and Ferryland, Newfoundland. (I'd never heard of any of them, and trust most of you haven't, either.) But as McLean hunkers down for a longish stay in each town, we come to know not just the residents of the place, but also its patchwork quilt, and how that history fits into the larger history of the times, including the separatist movement in Quebec, racial issues in Ontario, and more. McLean's book, published in 1993, doesn't reflect its age.

Anything that Jan Morris writes, I'll read, because of her incisive descriptions, her grasp of history, and her ability to pick just the right examples for any point she chooses to make. Even though **O Canada: Travels in an Unknown Country** is now almost two decades old, the descriptions she offers of ten Canadian cities—St. John's, Toronto, Montreal, Yellowknife, Banff, Saskatoon, Edmonton, St. Andrews, Ottawa, and Vancouver—will still make you want to go visit them.

Once I tell you the plot of **The Girls** by Lori Lansens, you might have to overcome a certain discomfort before you pick it up, but please don't let the subject matter—the story of conjoined twins Rose and Ruby Darlen—prevent you from reading what is one of the most humane, touching, and beautifully written books you'll read this or any other year.

Tom Allen's **Rolling Home: A Cross Country Railroad Memoir** is hard to find, but—especially if you're keen on travel by railroad, as I am—worth looking for. It was published a few decades ago, but it's still evocative, informative, and engaging.

Other books either by Canadians or about the country include those by Miriam Toews—my two favorites of her novels are **The Flying Troutmans** and **A Complicated Kindness**; for pure fun, take a look at Douglas Coupland's three volumes of **Souvenir of Canada** in which you'll find some iconic Canadiana by a native son: everything from "stubbies" to two-headed geese; two superb novels by Emily St. John Mandel—**Last Night in Montreal** and **The Singer's Gun**; the works of Paulette Jiles, whose fiction is not set in Canada but whose ability to bring a place and characters to life shines through in such titles as **The Color of Lightning** (Texas) and **Enemy Women** (the America Civil War); mystery fans shouldn't miss the gripping novels of Giles Blunt, all set in Northern Ontario—my favorite is **Forty Words for Sorrow**; and don't forget Margaret Atwood, Alice Munro, and Robertson Davies.

CAVORTING THROUGH THE CARIBBEAN

The first thing you'll want to read before heading off to the land of sun and sea is the dictionary, to figure out how you're going to pronounce it: kar-ə-bē-ən or kə-ri-bē-ən. The first is widely used in the United States, while the latter is the preferred pronunciation when you're "in country." My advice is to pick one and stick with it, no matter where you are. I've gone with the second, for what it's worth.

Here are the countries I'm including in this section—Antigua, Cuba, the Dominican Republic, Haiti, Jamaica, Puerto Rico, and Trinidad and Tobago.

Antigua

Annie John by Jamaica Kincaid is a lovely coming-of-age novel. Though Annie John grows up on Antigua, I think the feelings she experiences are universal. Most of Kincaid's novels and short story collections deal with life in the West Indies.

Cuba

When I read **Three Trapped Tigers**, Guillermo Cabrera Infante's 1958 novel (and acknowledged masterpiece) in the one language I'm fluent in—English—I was sorely tempted to learn Spanish, just so I could read it in the original and experience it *in situ*, as it were, for so much of the wordplay and sense of fun must inevitably be lost in translation, no matter how excellent the translator(s)—in this case, Donald Gardner and Suzanne Jill Levine, in collaboration with the author. Even in English, though, the setting—pre-Revolutionary Cuba—came thoroughly alive. It's a must-read for anyone interested in Latin American literature or Cuban history and literature, as well as for fans of Borges, Nabokov (particularly **Pale Fire**), and Luis Fernando Verissimo. In fact, anyone taken with verbal high jinks will find this a delight.

Other books—fiction or nonfiction—that help us get a feel for this country only ninety miles from our border that has played such a major role in our national psyche include:

Washington Post reporter Michael Dobbs's riveting **One Minute to Midnight: Kennedy, Khrushchev, and Castro on the Brink of Nuclear War**. Although there have been numerous books written about 1961's Cuban Missile Crisis, it appears (from a nonscientific survey that I did recently among friends and family) that few people remember the details of an event that, along with the 1940s Berlin blockade and resulting airlift, demonstrated the political realities of a post-war, Cold War world.

Rachel Kushner's multilayered novel **Telex from Cuba** offers a portrait of Cuba in the years culminating in 1958's revolution, using a multiplicity of voices and viewpoints to describe the social and political realities during the decades-long setting of the American sun over the island. The writing, filled with memorable phrases and descriptions, carries the reader along effortlessly.

In 1970 Mexican journalist Alma Guillermoprieto spent six months teaching modern dance in Cuba. Her story, told in **Dancing with Cuba: A Memoir of the Revolution**, explores not just her life and career, but also the history of her "adopted" country and the revolution she supported.

NPR reporter Tom Gjelten's fascinating history of Cuba is described through the experiences of five generations of the Bacardi (think rum) family in **Bacardi and the Long Fight for Cuba: The Biography of a Cause**.

An excellent history of the early military involvement of the United States in Cuba can be found in Evan Thomas's **The War Lovers: Roosevelt, Lodge, Hearst, and the Rush to Empire, 1898**.

Havana: Autobiography of a City is Alfredo José Estrada's hymn of love to his native city.

Dervla Murphy (whose name you'll encounter many times in the pages to come) describes her trips to Cuba in **The Island That Dared: Journeys in Cuba**.

And don't forget Graham Greene's unforgettable **Our Man in Havana**. It's both an entertaining satire of the spy genre and a picture of pre-Castro Cuba.

Dominican Republic

Julia Alvarez's historical novel **In the Time of the Butterflies** is a heartrending, fact-based story of the Mirabal sisters during the dictatorial reign of Trujillo. You can watch my interview with Alvarez at www.seattlechannel.org/videos/video.asp?ID=3030606.

Junot Díaz's **Drown** is a collection of harsh and beautiful stories set both in the D.R. and among the Dominican immigrants in New York; and you simply shouldn't miss his utterly remarkable novel, **The Brief Wondrous Life of Oscar Wao**, about a New Jersey teenager dreaming of becoming the Dominican Republic's J. R. R. Tolkien. If audio books are your thing, this is a good one to choose.

I don't usually like true crime—too scary to think that these things actually happened—but I found an exception to be J. B. Mackinnon's **Dead Man in Paradise: Unraveling a Murder from a Time of Revolution**, the story of the murder of the author's uncle, a missionary in the D.R.

Haiti

Edwidge Danticat's memoir **Brother, I'm Dying** will likely bring you to tears, as it did me. Danticat opens the book with a day in 2004 when she learns that she is pregnant and that her father, André, is dying of pulmonary fibrosis. These two events, one happy and the other tragic, bracket Danticat's story of two brothers—her father, who decided to leave Haiti for the possibilities of a better life in New York, and her uncle, Joseph, her "second father," who chose to remain in Haiti.

It's not easy to find a happy book about Haiti, but Danticat's **After the Dance: A Walk Through Carnival in Jacmel, Haiti** fills that particular bill.

While I don't suppose you could call Tracy Kidder's **Mountains Beyond Mountains: The Quest of Dr. Paul Farmer, a Man Who Would Cure the World** particularly cheerful, it is both insightful and inspiring. You can watch my interview with Kidder at www.seattlechannel.org/videos/video.asp?ID=3031003.

If you want a little background, and/or have a particular interest in voodoo or Zora Neale Hurston, try her fascinating **Tell My Horse: Voodoo and Life in Haiti and Jamaica**, an account of her experiences learning voodoo practices in those countries during the 1930s.

Jamaica

Margaret Cezair-Thompson's novels **The True History of Paradise** and **The Pirate's Daughter** both offer compelling portraits of people living in this island nation.

The Jamaican American Colin Channer is a writer not to miss. I first discovered his work in **Iron Balloons: Hit Fiction from Jamaica's Calabash Writer's Workshop**, which he edited. Although **The Girl with the Golden Shoes** is set on a fictional Caribbean island, it's pretty clearly Jamaica. The stories in his collection **Passing Through** have a sultry beauty.

The Rastafarians by Leonard E. Barrett is an accessible history of the religious movement that began in Ethiopia and traveled to the Caribbean. It's a valuable introduction for those of us unfamiliar with its history, influences, and practices. Even though I am not a particular fan of Bob Marley's music (and he's the one who is most responsible for bringing the religion to the attention of music lovers worldwide), I found Barrett's book captivating.

And don't forget all of Andrea Levy's novels, including **Fruit of the Lemon**, **Small Island**, and her newest, **The Long Song**, set during the last years of slavery on the island.

Puerto Rico

Steven Torres writes a great series of mysteries set in a small town in Puerto Rico. The first is **Precinct Puerto Rico**, but there's no real need to read them in order.

I found **The Noise of Infinite Longing: A Memoir of a Family—and an Island** by Luisita López Torregrosa to be a mesmerizing account of growing up not only bilingual, but bicultural.

Rosario Ferré's early novels were written in Spanish, but she then turned to writing directly in English. Her second novel in English is **Eccentric Neighborhoods**; it offers a panoramic view of Puerto Rico as seen through the lives of one particular family.

Love and revolution in the 1950s are at the heart of **Captain of the Sleepers**, a novel by Mayra Montero. It's translated by Edith Grossman, who's one of, if not the, foremost translators of works from Spanish to English.

For those interested in Puerto Rico's colonial past, don't miss Edgardo Rodríguez Juliá's difficult (in the same way Borges is difficult) but exhilarating (in the same way Borges is exhilarating) novel, **The Renunciation**.

The lives of five generations of African Puerto Rican women are explored in **Daughters of the Stone** by Dahlma Llanos-Figueroa.

In Hunter S. Thompson's **The Rum Diary: The Long Lost Novel**, we get an exuberant picture of the drinking life in Puerto Rico in the 1950s.

Trinidad and Tobago

Noir mystery fans shouldn't miss **Trinidad Noir**, part of the Noir series published by Akashic Books. This one is edited by Lisa Allen-Agostini and Jeanne Mason. Dark, dark, dark, or should I say to better effect: noir, noir, noir.

Earl Lovelace's **Salt** shows the effects of colonialism on Trinidadian society and explores the diversity of its populace. But this is definitely not a humorless treatise—it's instead a novel that's alive with people and ideas; a must-read for anyone interested in Trinidadian history and culture.

Trinidad's Nobel Prize–winning writer V. S. Naipaul turns to nonfiction in **The Loss of El Dorado: A Colonial History**. Fiction readers won't want to miss Naipaul's novels that are set in his birthplace—**The Mystic Masseur** and **A House for Mr. Biswas** are my two favorites of his early novels. You might want to read his own writing before you tackle his biography: **The World Is What It Is: The Authorized Biography of V. S. Naipaul** by Patrick French. I usually think it's better to get to know a person's writings before you meet him or her in person.

I've also enjoyed the novels of Elizabeth Nunez, especially **Bruised Hibiscus** and **Anna In-Between**.

And the Others . . .

Don't forget the other Caribbean Islands and their authors, including St. Lucia's Derek Walcott, who won the Nobel Prize in 1992. Try **Omeros**, a retelling of Homer that is set primarily in the waters of the Caribbean. And Maryse Condé writes about her grandmother's life on the island of Marie-Galante, a dependency of Guadeloupe, in **Victoire**. The author calls this mix of family history and fiction a "reconstitution." Whatever you call it—novel, biography, or a combination of the two—it's one of the best depictions of island life.

CHESAPEAKE BAY

I went to college in Annapolis, Maryland, and still remember how beautiful the Chesapeake Bay area was. Here are some books that give you a sense of its appeal, as well as making clear that beauty is often only skin deep, and the ecology of the place (both natural and man made) doesn't make one sanguine about its future.

Beautiful Swimmers: Watermen, Crabs, and the Chesapeake Bay by William Warner

Chesapeake by James Michener

An Island Out of Time: A Memoir of Smith Island in the Chesapeake by Tom Horton, who reported on environmental issues for the *Baltimore Sun* newspaper

Mason's Retreat, a novel by Christopher Tilghman

Skipjack: The Story of America's Last Sailing Oystermen by Christopher White

Song Yet Sung, a historical novel by James McBride

The Tidewater Tales: A Novel and **The Development** by John Barth

The Waterman: A Novel of the Chesapeake Bay by Tim Junkin

CHINA: THE MIDDLE KINGDOM

I n the thirteenth century, the great traveler Marco Polo supposedly spent seventeen years with the emperor Kublai Khan. In Polo's memoir, **The Description of the World**, he describes Kublai Khan's magnificent palace. Or at least some scholars think he is describing what he saw—others believe that Polo was never really in China at all and simply concocted his description from merchants and others that he met along the Silk Road. We don't have to decide here whether or not Polo actually went to China and wrote about it—enough other people did to keep us reading for years, if not decades and lifetimes. In fact, books about the Middle Kingdom could probably fill *Book Lust To Go*, so I had to be very picky about what I included. Here then, in alphabetical order by author (and including both fiction and nonfiction, old and new), is where I'd begin my reading.

> Joe Bennett's **Where Underpants Come From: From Checkout to Cotton Field: Travels Through the New China and Into the New Global Economy** (I've also seen editions with a slightly different subtitle.)
> Isabella Bird's **The Yangtze Valley and Beyond: An Account of Journeys in China, Chiefly in the**

Province of Sze Chuan and Among the Man-tze of the Somo Territory

Iris Chang's **The Rape of Nanking: The Forgotten Holocaust of World War II** (gut-wrenchingly painful subject, handled with dignity)

Leslie T. Chang's **Factory Girls: From Village to City in a Changing China**

Da Chen's two memoirs: **Colors of the Mountain** and **Sounds of the River**

Shen Congwen's **Border Town** (a novel set before the Chinese Revolution and originally published in 1934)

Fuchsia Dunlop's **Shark's Fin and Sichuan Pepper: A Sweet-Sour Memoir of Eating in China** (great cover, too)

Gretel Ehrlich's **Questions of Heaven: The Chinese Journeys of an American Buddhist**

Emily Hahn's **China to Me**

Peter Hessler's three marvelous books: **River Town: Two Years on the Yangtze**; **Oracle Bones: A Journey Between China's Past and Present**; and **Country Driving: A Journey from Farm to Factory** (It's in the latter that Hessler coins the phrase "sinomapped" for those frequent times when his out-of-date book of driving maps led him to dead ends, nonexistent roads, and other untenable situations.)

Ha Jin's stories, collected in **Ocean of Words** and **A Good Fall**

Lincoln Kaye's **Cousin Felix Meets the Buddha: And Other Encounters in China and Tibet**

Yiyun Li's **The Vagrants**

Jen Lin-Liu's **Serve the People: A Stir-Fried Journey Through China**

Rosemary Mahoney's **The Early Arrival of Dreams: A Year in China**

W. Somerset Maugham's **The Painted Veil**

Zachary Mexico's **China Underground**

Kirsty Needham's **A Season in Red: My Great Leap Forward into the New China**

Jiang Rong's novel **Wolf Totem**

Jonathan Spence's **The Search for Modern China**, a solid yet readable history of the country that covers the sixteenth century to 1989

Jonathan Tel's **The Beijing of Possibilities** is a collection of stories set just before the 2008 Olympic games that—despite their surrealism and Italo Calvinoist tendencies (that's a compliment, actually)—depict Beijing in all its contradictory glory and shame.

Among the other plusses of Colin Thubron's **Shadow of the Silk Road**—an intricate weaving of history, sociology, philosophy, and contemporary events along a seven-thousand-mile journey—there's one brilliant sentence that I felt summed up modern China—that is, China of the twenty-first century: "All at once the future had grown more potent than the past." Those dozen words lead one in so many different directions: the Cultural Revolution, the life and death of dynasties, Islam, Buddhism, the Internet; they offer so much to think about. And don't miss Thubron's other great travel book about this country, **Behind the Wall: A Journey Through China**.

J. Maarten Troost's **Lost on Planet China: The Strange and True Story of One Man's Attempt to Understand the World's Most Mystifying Nation, Or How He Became Comfortable Eating Live Squid**

Robert Van Gulik's Judge Dee mysteries (set in the T'ang Dynasty), especially **The Chinese Bell Murders** and **The Chinese Maze Murders**

Simon Winchester's **The River at the Center of the World: A Journey up the Yangtze and Back in Chinese Time**

Jan Wong's **Beijing Confidential: A Tale of Comrades Lost and Found**

Lijia Zhang's **"Socialism Is Great!": A Worker's Memoir of the New China**

For a readable account of the Great March, which ultimately led to the victory of the Chinese Communists against the Nationalist army, take a look at Dean King's **Unbound: A True Story of War, Love, and Survival**.

If you're willing to add a little fantasy to your historical fiction, check out Guy Gavriel Kay's most wonderful **Under Heaven**, which takes place during the period of China's T'ang Dynasty

from 618 to 970. You can watch my interview with Kay at www
.seattlechannel.org/videos/video.asp?ID=7030813.

CLIMB EV'RY MOUNTAIN

Most of these titles could have been placed in the first
section of this book, "A Is for Adventure," but it
seemed that since there are so many excellent books
on mountain climbing, they deserved their own section. I do have
to say, though, that of all my virtual travel moments, these were
among my most emotionally draining reading experiences.

Edward Whymper, who was the first person to summit the
Matterhorn, called what he did "mountain scrambling." He tells of
his success (at long last: there were several failures that preceded it)
in **Scrambles Amongst the Alps: In the Years 1860–69**. Somehow "scrambling" brings the whole idea of ascending a mountain
a little closer to the realm of possibility. Possibly.

Another book that re-creates the past in the world of mountain
climbing is **Early Days in the Range of Light: Encounters
with Legendary Mountaineers**. In it, Daniel Arnold retraces
famous climbs—from 1864 to 1931—in the Sierra Nevadas. Part
memoir, part biography, part nature study and adventure travel, this
book is filled with an appreciation of the achievements of early
climbers, whom we know about (if at all) by the mountains that
bear their names.

A memoir that also explores the history of mountain climbing is
former Supreme Court Justice William O. Douglas's **Of Men and
Mountains**.

For anyone interested in the whys, whens, whos, and hows of climbing in the Himalayas, **Fallen Giants: A History of Himalayan Mountaineering from the Age of Empire to the Age of Extremes** by Maurice Isserman and Stewart Weaver is the book to choose. Although I didn't find it dry reading, this is not really a book for the casual reader, but rather for someone really consumed by the topic.

Ed Viesturs, mountain climber and writer, joined forces with prolific author David Roberts to write **K2: Life and Death on the World's Most Dangerous Mountain**. K2, located in the Karakoram Range of northern Pakistan, is known among climbers as "the holy grail of mountaineering," and Viesturs and Roberts have compiled stories from six of the most intense and riveting climbing seasons in the mountain's relatively recent history—1938, 1939, 1954, 1986, and 2008.

Another book about K2 that I thoroughly enjoyed is Jennifer Jordan's **Savage Summit: The True Stories of the First Five Women Who Climbed K2, the World's Most Feared Mountain**. It's somewhat awe-inspiring (and more than somewhat scary) to read about the sacrifices these women made to fulfill their dreams of climbing K2.

James Salter is one of the twentieth century's best (and probably these days, most under-read) writers. If by chance you happen to meet another Salter fan, it's a sign that the friendship was meant to be. Although I was dazzled by the writing of both **Light Years** (fiction) and **Burning the Days** (memoir), I found his novel **Solo Faces** to be a fascinating character study and probably the best mountain climbing novel I've ever read. In it, he says:

The rock is like the surface of the sea, constant yet never the same. Two climbers going over the identical route will each manage in a different way. Their reach is not the same, their confidence, their desire. Sometimes the way narrows, the holds are few, there are not choices—the mountain is inflexible in its demands—but usually one is free to climb at will.

When John Harlin III was nine years old, his good-looking, fearless father, known among the mountain climbing community as "the blond god," died on the north face of the Eiger, one of the Swiss Alps. Breaking a promise to his mother not to follow in his father's climbing footsteps, John realized that he had to at least attempt to conquer the mountain on which his father died. **The Eiger Obsession: Facing the Mountain That Killed My Father** won't disappoint those who enjoy true adventures and climbing memoirs.

Robert Macfarlane's **Mountains of the Mind: Adventures in Reaching the Summit** explores in fluid, evocative prose what motivates climbers (including the author himself) to climb a mountain—almost any mountain.

In Georgina Howell's riveting biography, **Gertrude Bell: Queen of the Desert, Shaper of Nations** (mentioned in the Arabia Deserta section), there's a pulse-pounding account of one of Bell's ascents in the Alps.

Bree Loewen spent three years as a climbing ranger on Mount Rainier; she recounts the triumphs and tragedies in **Pickets and Dead Men: Seasons on Rainier**.

COMICS WITH A SENSE OF PLACE

Comics, with their blend of image and text, can create a strong sense of place. The emphasis on images gives birth to landscapes, dress, details of buildings, and a range of perspectives. The focus on text brings to life speech patterns and quick shots of brief and vivid descriptions. While the visual nature of comics demands that landscape is always part of the picture, sometimes comics become all about location, bringing a place to visual and textual life. Here are some fantastic comics that transport readers to another locale.

Much of Alison Bechdel's **Fun Home: A Family Tragicomic** takes place in Bechdel's family home (which she vividly details in her photo-realistic style), but the comic is also set, in part, in New York City, and Bechdel brings fine-grain detail to the skyline and streets.

From Hell, written by Alan Moore and drawn by Eddie Campbell, allows us to step into a vividly re-created world of London during the time of Jack the Ripper. Campbell's seething streets and watery lights can easily evoke pure terror in the jittery reader.

John Porcellino divides **Thoreau at Walden** into four seasons so that we can see Walden Pond in a series of clear and elegant lines.

The impressionistic text and images combine to evoke Thoreau's philosophy and the landscape that helped shape it.

Greg Rucka's two volumes of **Whiteout** are mysteries featuring U.S. Marshall Carrie Stetko, set in Antarctica. The illustrations are by Steve Lieber.

Joshua Neufeld introduces us to a variety of people in his splendid graphic novel, **A.D.: New Orleans After the Deluge**. It's viscerally moving and intellectually satisfying.

Using the medium of the graphic novel to great effect, Jason Lutes's **Berlin: City of Stones** and **Berlin: City of Smoke** offer a history of the city in a way that's accessible and yet mind-opening. All the benefits of a good novel are here: three-dimensional characters, a dynamic plot, and a well-drawn setting, and the pictures expand the story most satisfyingly. These two volumes were originally part of his ongoing comic book series, called, quite simply, **Berlin**.

Bryan Talbot's dazzlingly brilliant **Alice in Sunderland** explores the connections between Sunderland, Talbot's beloved hometown in the northeast corner of England, and another of his great loves, Lewis Carroll's **Alice in Wonderland**. He offers up a vivid history of the place from Roman times to the present; the accompanying illustrations include drawings, photos, and reproductions of newspaper articles, letters, and much more. Reading this was one of the richest experiences of my life.

Another author/illustrator to check out is Guy Delisle. His books include **Pyongyang: A Journey in North Korea**, **Burma Chronicles**, and **Shenzhen: A Travelogue From China**.

CONGO: FROM COLONIALISM
TO CATASTROPHE

My reading has not turned up too many native Congolese writers whose works are easily available in English. The one I found—whose writing is nicely reminiscent of Graham Greene—is Emmanuel Dongala (see below). But there are many good books available about this Central African nation whose history is bleak and violent, and whose present does not lead one to an optimistic view of its future.

Larry Devlin's **Chief of Station, Congo: Fighting the Cold War in a Hot Zone**

Emmanuel Dongala's **Little Boys Come from the Stars** (one of two novels on this list)

Che Guevara's **The African Dream: The Diaries of the Revolutionary War in the Congo**

Pagan Kennedy's **Black Livingstone: A True Tale of Adventure in the Nineteenth-Century Congo**

Daniel Liebowitz and Charles Pearson's **The Last Expedition: Stanley's Mad Journey Through the Congo**

Bryan Mealer's **All Things Must Fight to Live: Stories of War and Deliverance in Congo**

Redmond O'Hanlon's **No Mercy: A Journey into the Heart of the Congo**

Jeffrey Tayler's **Facing the Congo: A Modern-Day Journey into the Heart of Darkness**

W. T. Tyler's **The Consul's Wife** (the other novel on
this list)

Vanessa Woods's **Bonobo Handshake: A Memoir of
Love and Adventure in the Congo** (animal lovers
will really enjoy this)

CORFU

Who hasn't dreamed of running off to some sun-drenched island? Corfu is certainly a popular destination for dreamers.

One of the best reasons for making Corfu your island destination (especially if you're a reader) is that it's the setting of one of the funniest books ever written: **My Family and Other Animals** by Gerald Durrell. Its sequels, while maybe not up to the joyful perfection of the first book, are no slouches, either: **Birds, Beasts, and Relatives** and **The Garden of the Gods** definitely carry on the humor.

But don't miss these other titles: while they may not have the bestiary that characterize Durrell's books, they all have their special charms.

Lawrence Durrell (yes, Gerald's sibling, although seemingly far less attached to animals than his brother) wrote **Prospero's Cell: A Guide to the Landscape and Manners of the Island of Corfu** (a little of it fiction, a little bit of it nonfiction).

Emma Tennant's **A House in Corfu: A Family's Sojourn in Greece** and **Corfu Banquet: A Memoir with Seasonal Recipes** will please both homebodies and foodies.

And how could I not include Mary Stewart's **This Rough Magic**? It's the best sort of romantic suspense, the kind that only Stewart could write. And, of course, it's set in Corfu.

CORNWALL'S CHARMS

Cornwall is at the southwestern tip of England, and for such a relatively small place it's a treasure trove for literarily inclined readers (perhaps especially romance readers).

Daphne du Maurier set many of her gothic novels in and around Cornwall, including **My Cousin Rachel** and **Rebecca**. I'll never forget the first lines of the former: "They used to hang men at Four Turnings in the old days. Not any more, though." Those sentences still send a shiver up my spine.

Malcolm MacDonald's **The Carringtons of Helston** is a good choice for readers who enjoy family sagas.

If what you love is a series of historical novels, you can't do much better than Winston Graham's Poldark series. These twelve novels are set in the eighteenth and nineteenth centuries. They need to be read in order, beginning with **Ross Poldark: A Novel of Cornwall 1783–1787** and ending (many months of reading later, I'm sure) with **Bella Poldark: A Novel of Cornwall 1818–1820**.

The evocative romance novels by Rosemary Aitken that I've read are all set in Cornwall, many of them in the village of Penvarris, including **The Silent Shore** and **Stormy Waters**; I'd also suggest **The Granite Cliffs**.

The plot of **Wings of Fire**, the second of the Charles Todd mysteries featuring World War I–veteran Detective Ian Rutledge of Scotland Yard, has Rutledge traveling to Cornwall to investigate some suspicious deaths.

Other Cornwall-set fiction includes the delightful **Harnessing Peacocks** by Mary Wesley; any in Philippa Carr's Daughters of England series—the ones I liked best (for no particular reason) are **The Gossamer Cord** and **We'll Meet Again**, numbers 18 and 19, respectively; **Penhallow**, a mystery by one of my very favorite novelists, Georgette Heyer; **Penmarric** by Susan Howatch; **Mistress of Mellyn** by Victoria Holt; **The Little Country** by Charles de Lint (some of it set in Cornwall, anyway); and Jill Paton Walsh's **The Serpentine Cave**. You might as well throw in the Arthurian saga by Mary Stewart, since many scholars believe Arthur was born in Cornwall: **The Crystal Cave**, **The Hollow Hills**, **The Last Enchantment**, and **The Wicked Day**.

As for nonfiction, Daphne du Maurier's **Vanishing Cornwall** is a winsome word picture of her adopted home. It is a must-read for any visitor.

CORSICA

The Mediterranean island of Corsica is probably best known as the birthplace of Napoleon Bonaparte, but here are some selections of Corsica-centered titles that have nothing to do with Napoleon.

There's a chapter on Corsica in Paul Theroux's **The Pillars of Hercules: A Grand Tour of the Mediterranean**. Here's how he describes the island:

> Corsica is famous for having its own fragrant odor—the herbaceous whiff of the *maquis*—lavender, honeysuckle, cyclamen, myrtle, wild mint and rosemary. . . . It smells like a barrel of potpourri, it is like holding a bar of expensive soap to your nose. The Corsican *maquis* is strong enough to clear your lungs and cure your cold.

Brian Bouldrey's **Honorable Bandit: A Walk Across Corsica** is much more than a travel book—there are sections on his life as a gay man, his family, and all the various and sundry folks he meets as he traverses the roads of the island.

In **The Rose Café: Love and War in Corsica**, John Hanson Mitchell describes the six months he spent in 1962 living on the island and working in a small café. As we meet the café's staff and its regular customers, we begin to learn—as Mitchell did—their varied experiences in World War II. Reading Mitchell's book is a way of reminding ourselves that the past is never really forgotten, never really gone, and seldom ameliorated.

DEFINITELY DETROIT

One of the best memoirs I've read about growing up in Detroit is Paul Clemens's **Made in Detroit**. Born in 1973, the year that Coleman Young became the first black mayor of the city, Clemens writes movingly and honestly about his experiences as a member of the ever-dwindling white minority in a rapidly collapsing city.

Loren Estleman's Amos Walker mystery series is set in Detroit. No need to read them in order: the most recent, and probably easiest to find, is **Sugartown**.

Detroit native Jeffrey Eugenides has a talent for knock-your-socks-off first lines. His wonderful first novel **The Virgin Suicides**, set in an exclusive suburb of Detroit, opens this way: "On the morning the last Lisbon daughter took her turn at suicide—it was Mary this time, and sleeping pills, like Therese—the two paramedics arrived at the house knowing exactly where the knife drawer was, and the gas oven, and the beam in the basement from which it was possible to tie a rope." And **Middlesex**, his second novel, which won the Pulitzer Prize, begins: "I was born twice: first, as a baby girl, on a remarkably smogless Detroit day in January of 1960; and then again, as a teenage boy, in an emergency room near Petoskey, Michigan, in August of 1974."

In **The Other Side of the River: A Story of Two Towns, a Death, and America's Dilemma**, Alex Kotlowitz explores issues of race and justice in two cities in the southwest part of Michigan: Benton Harbor and St. Joseph. Although this isn't, of course, exactly a Detroit book, it's such a terrific account (and I am such a Kotlowitz fan) that I had to include it here.

For anyone who grew up in Detroit, as I did, **The Art Student's War** by Brad Leithauser offers a way to travel back in time to the period during and after World War II, when the city hummed with energy and importance. And Leithauser's writing is magical.

Many of Elmore Leonard's thrillers take place in Detroit. And with a Leonard novel you're assured a bit of grit, a lot of snappy dialogue, and an appealing (if sometimes flawed) hero. Introduce yourself to his work with **City Primeval: High Noon in Detroit**.

Much of Philip Levine's poetry reflects his working-class Detroit roots. The collection of his that I most enjoy is **What Work Is**, but you can't go wrong with any of his collections.

Joyce Carol Oates set her National Book Award–winning novel **Them** in inner-city Detroit. It's the story of the Wendall family, from the post-Depression 1930s to the race riots of 1967.

EGYPT

Egypt's long and storied history has led to much good reading: Three especially useful and entertaining works of popular history about the region include Brian M. Fagan's **The Rape of the Nile: Tomb Robbers, Tourists, and Archaeologists in Egypt**; Nina Burleigh's **Mirage: Napoleon's Scientists and the Unveiling of Egypt**; and Barbara Mertz's **Temples, Tombs, and Hieroglyphs: A Popular History of Ancient Egypt**.

One of the best finds of all my reading for *Book Lust To Go* was Florence Nightingale's **Letters from Egypt: A Journey on the Nile, 1849–1850**. I am always hooked by books in the genre I call "letters home," and this was no exception. If reading these letters makes you want to find a really good biography of Nightingale (as it did for me), try (as I did) Mark Bostridge's **Florence Nightingale: The Making of an Icon**.

Another account of life in Eqypt is André Aciman's **Out of Egypt: A Memoir**, which tells the story of his eccentric family of Sephardic Jews from the turn of the twentieth century to the present.

A bit narrower in subject, but just as interesting, is Janet Soskice's **The Sisters of Sinai: How Two Lady Adventurers Discovered the Hidden Gospels**.

As for fiction, of course the first author you have to read is Naguib Mahfouz. I'd begin with the Cairo Trilogy, made up of **Palace Walk**, **Palace of Desire**, and **Sugar Street**. You could spend some serious reading time just perusing this Nobel Prize–winning author's novels.

Among newer titles, I very much enjoyed **The Blue Manuscript**, in which the author, Sabiha Al Khemir, weaves together the past and present as she portrays the history of a manuscript—from the scribe who produced it, to the archaeologists determined to locate it, to the collectors who covet it.

ENTERING ENGLAND

There were four sections in *Book Lust To Go* that I kept putting off writing until the last possible moment because they seemed so daunting to me. There is so much material to include on England (with or without including London), India, New York (city and state), and the Middle East that I remained unable to choose what to include until the manuscript-delivery deadline was edging dangerously close. And there were so many titles to choose from! I had to pick what I included very carefully indeed.

I discovered **The Intelligent Traveller's Guide to Historic Britain: England, Wales, the Crown Dependencies** by Phillip Axtell Crowl after I talked about armchair travel on the radio. Here's what a listener emailed me:

> Yes, the title sounds a bit pretentious, but I have found it to be a great guidebook for finding all the little places that you would never find on your own, or even know to look for. The book presents its material in two formats, by its place on the map and its place in history. My travels around Britain tend to be fairly free form, so I tend to go by location. If I am going from point A to point B, I can look at the book to see what I might find along the way. My discoveries have included ancient Celtic burial grounds and Roman baths. You almost need an Ordnance Survey map to find some of the places. The good spots tend to be down some narrow back road with a path through some farmer's field to get there. They don't make it on the standard AA maps.

When I tracked it down (it's out of print but is relatively easy to find used, or perhaps at your local library—it wasn't available at mine) I saw exactly what my correspondent meant. Crowl also wrote books on historic Ireland and historic Scotland.

I loved Ian Mortimer's **The Time Traveller's Guide to Medieval England: A Handbook for Visitors to the Fourteenth Century**. Any history fan should also enjoy this unique way of animating the past. Even though when I finished the book

I couldn't honestly say that I wished I lived in the fourteenth century (I value my Dial soap and iPhone a bit too much), I did wish I could pop back in time for a brief but enlightening visit.

A. A. Gill is a Scots-born columnist for the *London Sunday Times*. In **The Angry Island: Hunting the English** his essays are filled with biting, sometimes snarky commentary about the morals and mores of England.

London: The Biography by Peter Ackroyd is required reading for any traveler to England's capitol. But be forewarned: it's a hefty tome. On the plus side (an enormous plus) is Ackroyd's entirely engaging writing—there's nary a dull page or anecdote. Among Ackroyd's other books of useful fiction or nonfiction for the Britain-bound traveler are **Thames: The Biography** and **Albion: The Origins of the English Imagination**.

Some other excellent nonfiction titles include **The London Scene: Six Essays on London Life** by Virginia Woolf (the cover alone is worth the book's price); **The Coast Road: A 3,000 Mile Journey Round the Edge of England** by award-winning travel writer Paul Gogarty; **Mustn't Grumble** by Joe Bennett (native New Zealander wanders his adopted country); and **An Audience with an Elephant: And Other Encounters on the Eccentric Side** by Byron Rogers, a columnist for the *Sunday Telegraph* and *Guardian* papers—perfect for already-committed Anglophiles.

The Polite Tourist: Four Centuries of Country House Visiting by Adrian Tinniswood is an outstanding work of social history, made even better by the illustrations. After reading it I felt quite comfortable that I would know exactly how to behave should I ever have occasion to spend some time as a guest in a country house. Rounding out the list are **In A Fog: The Humorists' Guide to England**, edited by Robert Wechsler, which includes essays by Art Buchwald, Mark Twain, Paul Theroux, and Robert Benchley, among others; and **England for All Seasons** by Susan Allen Toth, characterized by the author's idiosyncratic enthusiasms about the country she loves to visit.

Anglophiliacs who love fiction are fortunate. I often think that nearly every third book in a library or bookstore's fiction collection is likely by a British writer and/or set somewhere in England.

Sarum: The Novel of England, London: The Novel, and **The Forest** (set in the New Forest, in the southern portion of the country) by Edward Rutherfurd are sometimes dismissed as being too fluffy to convey you across the Atlantic. But in fact they're detailed, painstakingly researched, and filled with interesting characters.

Here's a diverse group of other titles that I've thoroughly enjoyed in the last few years. Like the divine writing of Georgette Heyer, author Julia Quinn brings the British Regency period to life in her sparkling romances, filled with dashing gentleman and bright, saucy women. My current tell-everyone-I-know-about-it is **What Happens in London**, but there are many other Quinn confections to choose from; Sarah Waters's **The Night Watch**, set in World War II London; Susan Howatch's Starbridge series including, among others, **Glamorous Powers**, **Glittering Images**, and **Absolute Truths**; **The Road Home** by Rose Tremain; and anything by Elizabeth Jane Howard, especially the Cazalet Chronicles, consisting of **The Light Years**, **Marking Time**, **Confusion**, and **Casting Off**, spanning 1937–1938 through the end of World War II in the life of one British family.

ETHIOPIA, OR AS WE USED TO SAY, ABYSSINIA!

Tahir Shah's **In Search of King Solomon's Mines** is armchair travel writing at its finest: interesting characters (especially Samson, Shah's sometimes unwilling travel companion, a Christian Amhari who totes an enormous Bible wherever he goes), nice-sized splotches of history and geography (both Ethiopian and biblical), and most important, an appealing writer whose sense of humor is apparent right from the beginning of the trip and continues through even the most trying of times (Shah is jailed as a suspected spy in Ethiopia). After a visit to the Middle East, Shah, a native Afghani who grew up in England, found himself compelled to locate the mines of the biblical King Solomon, a journey that eventually took him throughout Ethiopia into the mostly illegal gold-mining camps, following in the footsteps of the legendary Frank Hayter, who explored Ethiopia in the 1920s. Hayter's three memoirs, all published in the 1930s, include **In Quest of Sheba's Mines**, **Gold of Ethiopia**, and **African Adventurer**.

Cutting for Stone, an irresistibly readable epic novel by Abraham Verghese, begins right after World War II, when Mary Joseph Praise, a devout young nun, travels from her home in Kerala, India, to Addis Ababa, Ethiopia, and finds work in a mission hospital there. On the stormy and difficult sea voyage over, she saves the life of a British doctor named Thomas Stone, who also winds up at Missing, as the hospital is known to everyone in Addis. (Coincidences like this occur often in epic novels: they make the plot hum.) Although much of the book is set in New York (and narrated by Mary Joseph

Praise's son, Marion), when I finished reading this, I wanted to take the next flight to Addis Ababa because the author brought the city to life as a dynamic and three-dimensional character in its own right.

Other books set in Ethiopia, both fiction and nonfiction, include:

Tim Bascom's **Chameleon Days: An American Boyhood in Ethiopia**

Philip Caputo's powerful novel **Horn of Africa**

Nicholas Clapp's **Sheba: Through the Desert in Search of the Legendary Queen** unravels the contradictory and complex tale of Sheba (of biblical Solomon and Sheba fame).

Thomas Keneally's novel **To Asmara**

Maaza Mengiste's moving and poetic novel **Beneath the Lion's Gaze**, set just before the violent 1974 revolution that ended the reign of Emperor Haile Selassie

Nega Mezlekia's **Notes from the Hyena's Belly: Memories of My Ethiopian Boyhood** interested me because it's set not in Addis Ababa, but rather in Jijiga, a small town on the eastern border of the country.

Wilfred Thesiger's **The Life of My Choice** (The great explorer and desert-lover was born in the country when it was still Abyssinia.)

Maria Thomas's **African Visas: A Novella and Stories** (Ironically, Thomas died while on a relief mission in Ethiopia in 1988.)

EXPLAINING EUROPE:
THE GRAND TOUR

The Grand Tour was almost a rite of passage in the eighteenth and nineteenth centuries. Here are some twentieth-century titles that give us an overview of today's Europe.

Bill Bryson's **Neither Here Nor There** recounts the backpacking tour around Europe more than two decades after Bryson and a friend traveled throughout Europe in the 1970s.

In Geert Mak's **In Europe: Travels Through the Twentieth Century**, the well-read and knowledgeable Dutch journalist roams across Europe in the last year of the twentieth century to assess its health by looking at its past, its present, and its future.

Another look at Europe comes from British writer John Gimlette, winner of the Shiva Naipal Memorial Prize and the Wanderlust Travel Writing Award, in **Panther Soup: Travels Through Europe in War and Peace**. Think of this and Mak's book as the perfect Grand Tour without leaving home.

For pure entertainment, try Tim Moore's **The Grand Tour: The European Adventure of a Continental Drifter** and Alice Steinbach's **Without Reservations: The Travels of an Independent Woman**.

Although they don't write about twentieth-century travel, I can't resist including Brian Dolan's smart and stylish **Ladies of the Grand Tour: British Women in Pursuit of Enlightenment and Adventure in Eighteenth-Century Europe**, as well as one of the most loved books of the nineteenth century—it was in its twenty-fourth revised edition in 1860—**Views Afoot; or,**

Europe Seen with Knapsack and Staff by Bayard Taylor. What a fabulous adventure it would be to follow in his footsteps, almost 150 years later.

EXPLORERS

It takes a special kind of person to set off for the "here be dragons" section of the map. I'm not sure I'd like to spend much time with people of that personality type—that kind of one-directional determination makes me a bit anxious. It's certainly a quality that real explorers must have in spades. But gosh, these men and women are fun to read about. Here are some of my favorite biographies; there's nary a dull one in the bunch.

Barrow's Boys: A Stirring Story of Daring, Fortitude, and Outright Lunacy by Fergus Fleming includes enthralling mini-biographies and backstories of many of the nineteenth-century explorers who filled in the blank places on the map and added to Britain's empire. If you enjoy this, take a look at Fleming's **Off the Map: Tales of Endurance and Exploration**.

Another book you won't want to miss is Nathaniel Philbrick's **Sea of Glory: America's Voyage of Discovery: The U.S. Exploring Expedition**. Six vessels and hundreds of crewmen set out to discover all there was to know about the Pacific Ocean. These voyages, known more familiarly as the "Ex Ex," added immeasurably to America's scientific knowledge and almost incidentally brought back hundreds of artifacts (many of which ended up in the Smithsonian Museum).

Others to add to your reading list include **Spinsters Abroad: Victorian Lady Explorers**, Dea Birkett's vivid account of stereotype-shattering nineteenth-century women like Mary Kingsley, Isabella Bird, Mary Gaunt, and Marianne North (neither of the last two I'd heard of before stumbling on this book in the travel section of a used bookstore a few years ago); Jason Roberts's **A Sense of the World: How a Blind Man Became History's Greatest Traveler** (despite the somewhat arguable subtitle, this tale of James Holman greatly merits reading); D'Arcy Jenish's **Epic Wanderer: David Thompson and the Mapping of the Canadian West**, a readable history of the great mapmaker that makes use of Thompson's journals and sketches to enhance the text; **Half Moon: Henry Hudson and the Voyage That Redrew the Map of the New World** by Douglas Hunter; Peter G. Mancall's **Fatal Journey: The Final Expedition of Henry Hudson**, which offers a plausible explanation for Hudson's disappearance; **Over the Edge of the World: Magellan's Terrifying Circumnavigation of the Globe** by Laurence Bergreen; and **A Land So Strange: The Epic Journey of Cabeza de Vaca** by Andrés Reséndez (a friend told me how difficult it was to put this down—she found it, as I did, a riveting tale).

There's more: **Ledyard: In Search of the First American Explorer** by Bill Gifford (John Ledyard was a friend of Thomas Jefferson's who left Dartmouth College, sailed with Captain Cook on his last trip, wandered through Siberia, and ended up pretty much unremarked and unremembered except by those who read Gifford's book); and Tim Jeal's **Stanley: The Impossible Life of Africa's Greatest Explorer**. The amount of infamy and fame surrounding the subject would have daunted all but the most determined—and excellent—biographer. (Jeal is both—you may want to check out some of his other books, as I did.)

Once you've finished the Jeal book, pick up Martin Dugard's **Into Africa: The Epic Adventures of Stanley and Livingstone** and Anthony Sattin's **The Gates of Africa: Death, Discovery, and the Search for Timbuktu**, a history of the African Association, founded in 1788 with the sole purpose of filling in the map of Africa by locating Timbuktu, finding the source of the Nile, and exploring the course of the Niger River (among much else, of course). And don't forget Giles Milton's delectable **The Riddle and the Knight: In Search of Sir John Mandeville, the World's Greatest Traveller**, in which the author tries to help the reader decide whether Mandeville accomplished all the great exploring feats he describes in his own writing or whether he is, quite simply, a teller of tall tales. Should there perhaps be a question mark at the end of Milton's title? (Columbus took Mandeville's words quite seriously, if that's any help in coming to your own conclusion.)

Then there's William Harrison's enthralling novel **Burton and Speke**, which tries to answer the question of whether it was Richard Burton or John Hanning Speke who first found the source of the Nile. It was really an unfair contest, because Speke died mysteriously the day before he was scheduled to publicly debate the subject with Burton, and Burton's reputation as an explorer made Speke's claim seem a bit specious. And yet, we'll never know . . .

FROLICKING IN FINLAND

My older daughter spent her senior year of high school as a foreign exchange student in Finland—she lived with a family in Rovaniemi, the capital of Arctic Lapland. When she was there I started reading all I could find that was set in that country, which at the time was not much. While there are still not shelves and shelves of books either set in Finland or written by Finnish authors and translated into English, at least there are a few more now than there were back then. Here are some I've enjoyed a lot, although the descriptions of Finnish winters might freeze your blood.

The one true armchair travel book I found was Robert M. Goldstein's **Riding with Reindeer**, which describes his solo bike trip from Helsinki to the Barents Sea. The maps are wonderful, and the photos—so often lacking in books of this sort—add to the book's appealing conversational tone.

The Palace of the Snow Queen: Winter Travels in Lapland by Barbara Sjoholm describes the history and lives of the Sami people, who have long made Lapland their home.

Two new mystery writers whose books are set in Finland are Jan Costin Wagner and James Thompson. **Ice Moon** is the first of Wagner's three novels available in English. James Thompson's first novel, **Snow Angels**, features Inspector Kari Vaara.

Techies will want to check out **Just for Fun: The Story of an Accidental Revolutionary**, Linus Torvalds's memoir of growing up in wintry Finland, how he developed the Linux operating system and became perhaps the major proponent of open source codes for computers. (Even non-techies might enjoy this book—I certainly did, and I would never call myself one, although I do have a love of gadgets in common with the Finnish people. Did you know, for example, that there are more cell phones per capita in Finland than any other country in the world?)

To get an overall history of the bloody battle between Finland and the Soviet Union in the early years of World War II, the best book I've found for the general reader is **A Frozen Hell: The Russo-Finnish Winter War of 1939–40** by William Trotter.

Monika Fagerholm's first novel, written after publishing two collections of short stories, is **Wonderful Women by the Sea**, which takes place in her native Finland. I especially loved Fagerholm's writing style and the way she developed her characters. Her newest novel, **The American Girl**, also set in Finland, is another first-rate example of her capacious talent.

Books by Finnish writers that are available in English include **The Year of the Hare** by Arto Paasilinna; Antti Tuuri's **The Winter War** (a historical novel set in World War II; the author won the Finlandia Prize for Literature in 1997); and Väinö Linna's **The Unknown Soldier**, plus what are possibly his most famous books, a trilogy that includes **Under the North Star**, **The Uprising: Under the North Star 2**, and **Reconciliation: Under the North Star 3.**

Lastly, Maile Chapman's **Your Presence Is Requested at Suvanto** is both creepy and difficult to put down; it's set in a convalescent hospital for women that's deep in rural Finland.

GALLOPING THROUGH THE GALAPAGOS

It would be silly, I think, to take a trip to the Galapagos and not take at least a gander at Charles Darwin's **The Voyage of the Beagle: Journal of Researches into the Natural History and Geology of the Countries Visited During the Voyage of H.M.S. Beagle Round the World** (there's an edition with a useful introduction by Steve Jones). Darwin visited the Galapagos in 1835, four years into his five-year journey. In his autobiography, written half a century later, Darwin declared that "The voyage of the *Beagle* has been by far the most important event in my life and has determined my whole career."

In **Pilgrim on the Great Bird Continent: The Importance of Everything and Other Lessons from Darwin's Lost Notebooks**, nature writer Lyanda Lynn Haupt offers a narrative account of the *Beagle's* journey and how influential it was to Darwin's later career—how it truly did, in fact, make him what he became.

Jonathan Weiner's **The Beak of the Finch** examines evolution in the light of the relatively rapid changes that take place in the beak size and shape of a species of bird known as Darwin's finches, found mainly in the Galapagos. It's wonderfully written, extremely readable, and a superb example of the best kind of popular science writing.

Three good novels featuring Darwin and/or the Galapagos are **The Evolution of Jane** by Cathleen Schine (which is not about Darwin at all, but takes place in the Galapagos); Harry Thompson's Man Booker Prize shortlisted novel **To the Edge of the World** (the main characters are the captain of the *Beagle* and his most famous passenger, Charles Darwin); and **Mr. Darwin's Shooter** by Roger McDonald, a remarkable novel about the young man whom Darwin's biographer Janet Browne described as "the unacknowledged shadow behind every triumph." At fifteen, Syms Covington joined the crew of the HMS *Beagle*; now an elderly man, Covington is overcome by the guilt he still feels in being part of a life's work that will challenge humanity's view of itself.

And if you get really interested in Darwin and his life, don't forget that Irving Stone, the grandfather of biographical fiction (best known for his novels about Michaelangelo and Vincent Van Gogh), also wrote **The Origin: A Biographical Novel of Charles Darwin**.

GUERNICA

Guernica is a small town in the Basque region of Spain. What most people know about the place is Pablo Picasso's magnificent painting, which depicts—as probably only Picasso could—the brutal destruction of the town by German Luftwaffe bombs on April 26, 1937. Here are two novels in which Guernica plays a part:

Dave Boling's **Guernica**
Lawrence Thornton's **Under the Gypsy Moon**

And here are two wonderfully readable works of nonfiction that describe the genesis of Picasso's famous painting:

Russell Martin's **Picasso's War: The Destruction of Guernica, and the Masterpiece That Changed the World**

Gijs van Hensbergen's **Guernica: The Biography of a Twentieth-Century Icon**

GUERNSEY: HISTORY IN FICTION

This British island located near France in the English Channel was occupied by the Germans during World War II. This event is a central plot point in these three excellent novels, all of which bring the island to life, especially during this particularly difficult time in its history:

Tim Binding's **Lying with the Enemy**

G. B. Edwards's **The Book of Ebenezer Le Page**

Mary Ann Shaffer and Annie Barrows's **The Guernsey Literary and Potato Peel Pie Society**

HAIL, COLOMBIA!

Colombia is, more than most countries, greater than the sum of its parts. What we hear about—murders, drug cartels, kidnappings, and government incompetence at best and wholesale law-breaking at worst—as well as other various and sundry unsavory events, do constitute part of the country's past and present. These incidents are clearly the subtext of the books mentioned here. Nonetheless, there's more to Colombia than those things.

Colombia's greatest writer is, of course, Nobel Prize–winner Gabriel García Márquez. In **News of a Kidnapping**, an example of exemplary journalism, García Márquez reports on the events following the U.S. signature on a treaty that allows for the extradition of Colombian citizens, when the leaders of the Medellín drug cartel decided to use extra-legal methods to change the minds (and the laws) of both governments. If after reading that book you want to learn more about García Márquez, take a look at **Living to Tell the Tale**, the first of his projected three memoirs, as well as Gerald Martin's **Gabriel García Márquez: A Life**.

Novels set in Colombia include Dalia Rabinovich's **Flora's Suitcase**, the story of a young married Jewish couple from Cincinnati who move to Colombia in the 1930s; **Tales from the Town of Widows** by James Cañón; and two books by Colombian writers: Alvaro Mutis's **The Adventures and Misadventures of Maqroll** and Juan Gabriel Vásquez's **The Informers**.

As for nonfiction, try these:

Ingrid Betancourt's memoir **Until Death Do Us Part: My Struggle to Reclaim Colombia** recounts the events surrounding her attempt to become president of Colombia (which included being kidnapped and held for more than six years). In the process of describing her experiences, she helps readers understand her complex country. Although there have been books contradicting some of the material in here (especially her behavior during the kidnapping ordeal), I think it's a valuable read.

Beyond Bogota: Diary of a Drug War Journalist in Colombia by Garry Leech is set against the eleven hours he was "detained" by FARC, a guerilla group in Colombia.

I'll read anything by Mark Bowden—his writing is crisp and his subjects are fascinating. In **Killing Pablo: The Hunt for the World's Greatest Outlaw**, he describes the efforts of U.S. intelligence and other agencies to capture drug kingpin Pablo Escobar, who was at the time one of the most powerful cocaine traffickers.

Journalist Silvana Paternostro's **My Colombian War: A Journey Through the Country I Left Behind** provides an excellent and personal narrative history of the author's native country.

HAWAII

My father's brother served in the U.S. Army in Hawaii in the early 1930s, and to the end of his life talked about its physical beauty. It's true that the countryside could hardly have been more lush, but—as can be seen from the books described here—the history of the islands is filled with more than a little tragedy. So for a well-rounded picture of Hawaii, both its past and its present, take a look at these books.

Fiction

James Michener's **Hawaii** is probably the first book that comes to mind when you're thinking of what to read about the islands, but it shouldn't be the last.

Earl Derr Biggers wrote only six Charlie Chan mysteries, but the Chinese American detective is an iconic figure in the mystery canon. Try **House Without a Key**, set in Hawaii, to get a sense of both the place and the detective.

Alan Brennert has written two vibrant novels about the islands. **Moloka`i** is the story of a young girl with leprosy who spends her life in exile on the island of Molokai. It's perhaps especially relevant now since Father Damien, a Belgian priest who devoted his life to working with Molokai citizens who had Hansen's disease, was canonized by the Catholic Church in 2009. (If you find the subject matter of this novel intriguing, take a look at John Tayman's moving and informative **The Colony: The Harrowing True Story of the Exiles of Molokai**.) Brennert's second novel, **Honolulu**, is about a young Korean girl who comes to Honolulu as a "picture bride" in 1914.

Yoshiko Uchida's **Picture Bride** also offers an excellent look at what life was like for the Japanese and Filipino workers on the island's plantation camps.

Other novels include **Name Me Nobody** by Lois–Ann Yamanaka (as well as her other works of fiction); Lee A. Tonouchi's **da word** (yes, no initial capital letters), a collection of short stories written in pidgin; Jessica K. Saiki's **From the Lanai and Other Hawaii Stories**; James Houston's **Bird of Another Heaven**; Randy Sue Coburn's **A Better View of Paradise**; and the novels of Hawaii-born Kiana Davenport. I've never forgotten reading her very first novel, **Shark Dialogues**, a history of Hawaii as seen through the lives of four generations of a family, and have found her later novels—**House of Many Gods** and **Song of the Exile**—to be equally good.

Memoirs

Isabella Bird's **Six Months in the Sandwich Islands: Among Hawai`i's Palm Groves, Coral Reefs, and Volcanoes** is a series of letters written in 1871 to her sister, full of wonderful descriptions of the world of Hawaii before western culture so dramatically altered it.

In Lucinda Fleeson's **Waking Up in Eden: In Pursuit of an Impassioned Life on an Imperiled Island**, a journalist from Philadelphia takes a job with Hawaii's National Tropical Botanical Garden on the island of Kauai. This is an excellent choice for eco-readers.

Along with her own story, Lili`uokalani, the last queen of Hawaii, relates her country's tragic history in **Hawai`i's Story**. This should be required reading for anyone contemplating a trip there.

And don't neglect Garrett Hongo's **Volcano: A Memoir of Hawai`i**; Barack Obama's **Dreams from My Father: A Story of Race and Inheritance**; Susanna Moore's **Light Years: A Girlhood in Hawai`i**; and Tara Bray Smith's **West of Then: A Mother, a Daughter, and a Journey Past Paradise**.

HIKING THE (FILL IN THE BLANK) TRAIL

These are books about those intrepid souls who attempt to go from one end of a long, long trail to the other, carrying their packs up and over mountain passes, fording rivers, and subsisting on beef jerky and varieties of freeze-dried food. As I've learned from the books mentioned here, this group of hardy souls are known as "thru-hikers." You can usually tell who they are by their lean looks, their sometimes mildewed appearance (and odor), their insatiable hunger when they're taking one of their rare rest days, and, when it's all done, their well-deserved air of having finished a particularly onerous task.

The four major long-distance trails in the Americas are the Pacific Crest, the Appalachian, the Continental Divide, and the longest of all, the American Discovery Trail, which is more than 6,800 miles long and crosses fifteen states. How (or why) do people attempt these hikes? Read on.

When Dan White and his girlfriend, Melissa, decide to give up their newspaper jobs in Connecticut and walk the 2,650 miles of the formidable Pacific Crest Trail, which stretches from Mexico to British Columbia, through desert and rain forest, they have no idea what they've let themselves in for. As described in **The Cactus Eaters: How I Lost My Mind—and Almost Found Myself—on the Pacific Crest Trail**, their friends can't understand why they're doing it and their parents fear that they won't survive the experience. After vicariously sharing the couple's experiences with—among other things—exhaustion, sunstroke, giardia, bears, equipment malfunctions, blisters, hallucinations, and a particularly painful and unusual encounter with a cactus, readers will simultaneously applaud their determination to keep going and probably question their sanity.

Barbara Egbert's **Zero Days: The Real-Life Adventure of Captain Bligh, Nellie Bly, and 10-year-old Scrambler on the Pacific Crest Trail** relates her family's seven months of adventures on the trail. I particularly enjoyed reading the excerpts she includes

affected Will Truesdale, an enigmatic British chauffeur to a wealthy Hong Kong businessman. Lee keeps the plot moving quickly while forcing us to consider the moral ambiguities that face people trying to survive during wartime, and to ask ourselves just how much we would compromise of our beliefs and our sense of right and wrong in order to live.

Mrs. Pollifax, the fictional (and under very deep cover: a dithery elderly woman with a penchant for unusual hats) CIA operative, arrives in Hong Kong to do some sleuthing in Dorothy Gilman's novel **Mrs. Pollifax and the Hong Kong Buddha**.

The Honourable Schoolboy is the only book by John le Carré that I loved the first time around but have never been able to bring myself to reread (because of what I perceived as its desperate sadness). It's the more-or-less sequel to **Tinker Tailor Soldier Spy** and is set partly in Hong Kong during the height of the Cold War.

Gail Tsukiyama's **Night of Many Dreams** takes place both during the Japanese occupation of Hong Kong in the 1940s and twenty-five years later. It's the story of Joan and Emma Lew, who are fourteen and nine when the book opens. As with all Tsukiyama's novels, you come to care deeply for the fate of her characters.

James Clavell's **Noble House**, the third (and maybe best) in a series that includes **Tai-Pan** and **Gai-Jin**, is an engrossing saga and a perfect way to get a sense of history with a fast-moving plot attached. Or a fast-moving plot with a lot of history included.

And definitely don't miss checking out these, as well: Christina Sunley's **The Tricking of Freya**; Jess Row's **The Train to Lo Wu: Stories**; Leo Ou-fan Lee's **City Between Worlds: My Hong Kong**; Paul Theroux's novel **Kowloon Tong**; **The Last**

Six Million Seconds, a thriller by John Burdett; Alice Greenway's **White Ghost Girls** (a novel); John Lanchester's **Fragrant Harbor**; and Martin Booth's memoir **Golden Boy: Memories of a Hong Kong Childhood**, set in the 1950s.

ICELAND

One of the things I remember best about the 1960s is that the cheapest way to fly to Europe from the United States was on Icelandair. The benefit of flying with them was that you got to stop in Iceland's capital, Reykjavik. So I've always been on the lookout for books set there. Here are some I've enjoyed.

The mysteries of Arnaldur Indridason are fine examples of police procedurals. It's probably best to read them in order (or at least as much as we can, because not all of them have been published in the United States), beginning with **Jar City**. Unlike many police procedural series, we don't learn much about the personal lives of the detectives, but the main policeman, Erlendur Sveinsson, is (appropriately for the climate) generally dejected, and his relationship with his kids (with whom he evidently gave up all contact when he divorced) is awful (although it improves slowly throughout the series). Optimistic readers can see hope on the horizon (family-wise, if generally not for a society that seems on the brink of anger and despair) in **The Draining Lake** and **Arctic Chill**.

Yrsa Sigurdardóttir is the author of another crime series: **Last Rituals** and **My Soul to Take** both feature lawyer Thóra Gudmundsdóttir.

Bill Holm's **The Windows of Brimnes: An American in Iceland** describes how a Minnesotan moves to Iceland (for a part of every year) in order to explore his Icelandic heritage.

Two other books set in Iceland include Halldor Laxness's early twentieth–century saga, **Independent People** and **Iceland: Land of the Sagas** by Jon Krakauer and David Roberts. Lawrence Millman's **Last Places: A Journey in the North** has a good chapter on Iceland (along with sections on Greenland, Labrador, and the Faraoe Islands).

IN THE FOOTSTEPS OF . . .

If you're unsure of exactly where you want to travel, one way to decide is to pick a traveler of the past and follow in his or her footsteps. My thanks to these authors who did exactly that, and thus gave me many pleasurable hours of reading.

Any traveler with a good sole (sorry!) won't want to miss meeting one of the greatest travelers ever: Ibn Battutah, or more familiarly, IB. His full name is Abu Abdullah Muhammad Ibn Abdullah Al Lawati Al Tanji Ibn Battutah. (You may see his very last name spelled without a final "h" in some of the books and articles about him.) He was born at the beginning of the fourteenth century in what is now Tangier, made his pilgrimage to Mecca when he was twenty-one, and then simply never stopped traveling. In two of the most delightful books I've ever encountered, Arabic scholar and noted travel writer Tim Mackintosh-Smith recounts his journey following in the footsteps of the great traveler. The first is **Travels with a Tangerine: From Morocco to Turkey in the Footsteps**

of Islam's Greatest Traveler, in which Mackintosh-Smith duplicated the first half of IB's trip. These two travelers—Battutah and Mackintosh-Smith—separated by more than six hundred years and different cultures, are terrific companions: it appears that neither ever got bored, nor met someone he didn't enjoy talking with, and each approached every new day as a great adventure. The pleasure continues in **The Hall of a Thousand Columns: Hindustan to Malabar with Ibn Battutah**.

William Dalrymple describes how he traveled the same journey as Marco Polo—from the Church of the Holy Sepulchre in Jerusalem to Xanadu, which was Emperor Kublai Khan's summer capital (a not-easy overland trek that covered, all told, about twelve thousand miles)—in **In Xanadu: A Quest**. What I most enjoyed was how Dalrymple wove Polo's accounts with his own experiences along the way.

Tim Butcher became obsessed (I don't think that's too strong a term) with African explorer H. M. Stanley, and decided to replicate his dangerous 1864 journey mapping the Congo River. In **Blood River: A Journey to Africa's Broken Heart**, he not only describes the immediate problems he encounters on his trip (corrupt officials, a war that won't end, trouble in the adjoining countries that inevitably seeped into the Congo), but also gives the armchair traveler a history of this troubled nation, once known as the Belgian Congo, and now the DRC, the Democratic Republic of the Congo.

In **Chasing Che: A Motorcycle Journey in Search of the Guevara Legend**, Patrick Symmes retraces Che's 1952 journey over the back roads of South America. While describing his own

Most books about the Inside Passage focus on the journey up to Alaska. **The Sea Runners** by Ivan Doig starts in Sitka and heads south. Based on an actual incident from 1853, Doig's novel describes the perilous trip of four indentured servants who escape a Russian work camp in a stolen canoe and manage to paddle over a thousand miles to Astoria, Oregon.

Another author who evokes the spirit of the Inside Passage is Susan Vreeland; in **The Forest Lover** she imaginatively re-creates the world of Canadian artist Emily Carr. Carr spent her entire career trying to capture the spirit of the vast forests and native villages of British Columbia in her books and paintings.

Speaking of vast forests, don't miss John Vaillant's **The Golden Spruce: A True Story of Myth, Madness, and Greed**, which relates the haunting true story of Grant Hadwin, a logger/activist in the Queen Charlotte Islands who during a bizarre rage destroyed a unique "golden" spruce that had been sacred to the Haida Indians. No other recent story I know evokes the majestic scale of the forests along the coast of British Columbia.

Many cruise ships end their trips in Haines. For a good picture of what it's like to live in one of Alaska's smaller cities, try **If You Lived Here I'd Know Your Name: News from Small-Town Alaska** and **Take Good Care of the Garden and the Dogs: Family, Friends, and Faith in Small-Town Alaska** by Heather Lende.

Last but not least, what would a journey be without a bit of history amidst a mystery? In **The Big Both Ways** John Straley creates a picture of the Inside Passage in the mid-1930s, as a restless logger gets mixed up in a murder investigation involving a union organizer on the lam from the cops.

IRAN

There's no way she would remember this conversation, but when I met author Elaine Sciolino in 2000, shortly after her book **Persian Mirrors: The Elusive Face of Iran** was published, she urged me to visit the country. Sciolino enthusiastically described the warmth of its citizens, which persisted despite any restrictions their government might impose. It's been a decade since we met and I've yet to go to Iran, except through my readings of these books.

In **To See and See Again**, Tara Bahrampour describes her experiences growing up in Iran as the daughter of an Iranian Muslim father and a Jewish American mother. In the wake of the Islamic Revolution the author and her family left the country, and returned some fifteen years later for what would be the first of a number of visits.

Another excellent memoir is Terence Ward's **Searching for Hassan: A Journey to the Heart of Iran**, about an American family, once stationed in Iran, who returns to the country two decades after the revolution to search for the young servant boy they left behind when escaping the turbulence of the uprising.

After publishing **Reading Lolita in Tehran**, Azar Nafisi wrote **Things I've Been Silent About: Memories of a Prodigal Daughter**, a revealing autobiography that offers readers a much more complete picture of the author than was provided by her first book. I often felt while I was reading it that I was in the presence of someone who was slowly tearing a scab off a wound that was not yet completely healed, leaving it still bleeding and painful; I can

IRELAND: BEYOND JOYCE, BEHAN, BECKETT, AND SYNGE

Let's not start with James Joyce and just say we did, okay? Or, if we must, how about **A Portrait of the Artist As a Young Man**? Or his collection of stories, **Dubliners**. (I think I should take a course in **Ulysses** and **Finnegans Wake** before I include them here.) In fact, let's just get Brendan Behan, Samuel Beckett, and John Synge out of the way in this first paragraph. They're the classic Irish writers, and no more need be said. In any event, there are plenty of other books to read before venturing to the Ould Sod.

Does anyone read J. P. Donleavy's **The Ginger Man** any more? I certainly hope so, because it's probably one of the funniest, raciest, and most outrageous novels you'll ever encounter. Donleavy, an Irish American, moved to Ireland permanently after World War II. His **Ireland: In All Her Sins and in Some of Her Graces** is partly an autobiography and partly a tribute to his adopted country and a way of life no longer to be found. So, in honor of Donleavy, hoist a pint of Guinness stout and have a look.

William Trevor is the perfect writer for those readers who savor the language of a book, who read slowly to hear the words unspool in their minds. You can't go wrong with any book by him—they're all beautiful and sad—but I thought **Love and Summer**, short-listed for the Man Booker Prize, was one of his best. Other novels to try are the Whitbread Award–winning **Fools of Fortune** and **The Story of Lucy Gault**, which was shortlisted for both the Man Booker and the Whitbread Award. His short story collection **Cheating at Canasta** would be a fine introduction to his style, subjects, and way of looking at the world.

Nuala O'Faolain's memoir **Are You Somebody?: The Accidental Memoir of a Dublin Woman** offers an insightful (and painfully honest) portrait of growing up female in a society that's often hostile to women struggling for self-identity. And her novel **My Dream of You** incorporates Irish history and mores into its plot.

Travel writer David Yeadon's **At the Edge of Ireland: Seasons on the Beara Peninsula** portrays the beauty of this out-of-the-way, relatively nontouristy section in the southwest of the country.

And grab a handful of these novels to read: Edward Rutherfurd's **The Princes of Ireland** and **The Rebels of Ireland** (as might be guessed by the titles, these are historical novels); Frank Delaney's series of novels that consider Ireland's experiences in the twentieth century, such as **Ireland, Tipperary, Shannon**, and **Venetia Kelly's Traveling Show**; Stuart Neville's **The Ghosts of Belfast** (an unrelenting thriller); Booker Prize–winner Sebastian Barry's novels, including **The Secret Scripture**; Maeve Binchy's **Circle of Friends** and **The Scarlet Feather**; **The Best of Frank O'Connor**, which offers a sampling of this fine writer's fiction and nonfiction; Anne Enright's **The Gathering**; and Colm Tóibín's **The Heather Blazing**. In addition, the first and last parts of Tóibín's novel **Brooklyn** take place in a beautifully evoked small Irish town.

While it must be said that many Irish novelists tend to write bleak but beautiful fiction, there are lots of sunny tales about traveling around the country. One of my favorites is **McCarthy's Bar: A Journey of Discovery in Ireland** by Pete McCarthy. What he's trying to discover, in his own delightfully irreverent way, are all the bars that share his name. There's also a similarly belly laugh–worthy sequel called **The Road to McCarthy**, which broadens the scope of his travels.

Two other entertaining armchair travel books are Edward Enfield's **Freewheeling Through Ireland** and Eric Newby's **Round Ireland in Low Gear**, the account of a delightful and leisurely journey.

Mysteries set in Ireland vary from contemporary to historical, from the mean streets of today to those during early medieval times. (Even if the streets of the latter weren't paved, they were plenty mean.) Here are two mystery series I've enjoyed over the years, although I've discovered that you need to be in very different moods to enjoy them. The first is Ken Bruen's gritty novels about Jack Taylor, all of which take place in Galway. The newest is **Sanctuary**; I don't think you absolutely must begin with the first, as each one is pretty self-contained. Then there's Peter Tremayne's novels about Sister Fidelma, a seventh-century nun. A good one to start with is **The Council of the Cursed**, although the first one, for those committed to reading the series in order, is **Absolution by Murder**. (In his nonfiction-writing life, Tremayne is the noted Celtic scholar Peter Berresford Ellis.)

A very readable history of the country is **How the Irish Saved Civilization: The Untold Story of Ireland's Heroic Role**

from the Fall of Rome to the Rise of Medieval Europe by Thomas Cahill.

IT SEEMED LIKE A GOOD IDEA AT THE TIME

Sometimes you can come up with what sounds like a brilliant idea for a trip, work out the details, buy the airline tickets or the equipment you need, set off with the highest of hopes, and then discover to your shock and dismay that—for reasons both large and small, both within your control and without it—maybe it wasn't quite as brilliant an idea as you thought. Or sometimes, though the going gets tougher than you ever imagined, the gain is worth the pain: you change and grow and learn something important about yourself. Or not. See what you think when you read these books.

Almost on the spur of the moment—mainly influenced by a paper placemat at an all-night IHOP in Providence, Rhode Island—Susan Jane Gilman and her friend Claire decide to spend the year after their 1986 graduation from Brown University traveling around the world. They're going to rough it: there are to be no first-class hotels, no three-star meals, no English-speaking countries, no travel agent itineraries for them. Their journey will begin in China, which has just opened its borders to foreign visitors. Alas, as you'll find in her honest and surprising memoir **Undress Me in the Temple of Heaven**, nothing goes as planned.

Jim Malusa is a botanist whose specialty is the biogeography of the plants of southern Arizona, so you wouldn't necessarily pick him as the go-to guy to write about a series of bike trips. Yet, as he describes in **Into Thick Air: Biking to the Bellybutton of Six Continents**, he spent parts of six consecutive years riding his trusty bicycle to the lowest spots of all six continents, overcoming everything from extreme weather to extreme insects, not to mention the possibility of land mines if he strayed off the road in Africa. It's clear that Malusa would be a fun guy to bike with—he has a knack for meeting interesting people, hearing some fascinating stories, and ending up in amazing places.

Tony Horwitz's **Baghdad Without a Map and Other Misadventures in Arabia** was written during the time he worked as a stringer in the Middle and Near East, while his wife, Geraldine, was working as Middle East correspondent based in Cairo for the *Wall Street Journal*. One of my favorite lines—pure Horwitz humor and insight—is this: "It is difficult to gaze in awe at the wonders of ancient Egypt with modern Egypt tugging so insistently at your sleeve."

W. Hodding Carter's **Westward Whoa: In the Wake of Lewis and Clark** and **A Viking Voyage: In Which an Unlikely Crew of Adventurers Attempts an Epic Journey to the New World** are worth a read.

IT'S CHILE TODAY

It's a bit surprising to me, but I couldn't find a lot of armchair reading devoted to Chile. The best travel account that I found was Sara Wheeler's **Travels in a Thin Country: A Journey Through Chile**, and it's a real treat. As I discovered, Chile is approximately 2,600 miles long and is nowhere more than 250 miles wide (its average width is 110 miles). Wheeler makes her way (mostly by hitchhiking, walking, or taking a bus) from the arid north to the islanded south. Before reading this, I never really considered visiting Chile; now it's on my list of must-see places.

It's important to understand that—Wheeler aside—books on Chile are suffused with the political history of the place: it runs like a deep river beneath the plot or subject of a book. The terrible years of the Pinochet dictatorship are sometimes in the foreground, sometimes in the background, but they are always there for the author (and us) to conjure up.

Isabel Allende's memoir **My Invented Country: A Nostalgic Journey Through Chile** and, of course, her novels, especially **The House of the Spirits**, offer a picture of Chile that's suffused with love (and a bit of magic).

Roberto Bolaño's **The Savage Detectives** takes place in many more places than the author's native Chile; it provides a stunning portrait of Latin American life and literature.

Ariel Dorfman's works include **Heading South, Looking North: A Bilingual Journey** and **Desert Memories: Journeys Through the Chilean North**.

Antonio Skármeta's novels **The Postman** (the great Chilean poet Pablo Neruda's postman relates his charming love story) and **The Dancer and the Thief** (set in contemporary Santiago) are not to be missed.

Gabriel García Márquez is not Chilean, of course, but rather Colombian. However, **Clandestine in Chile: The Adventures of Miguel Littin** is a totally satisfying work of journalism about only call ruefully humorous. (In fact, I am at this moment completely unable to think of a truly "funny" novel written by a native Japanese. Enlighten me, please, if you've read one.) The best *gaijin* accounts I've read include:

Jake Adelstein's **Tokyo Vice: An American Reporter on the Police Beat in Japan**

Dave Barry's **Dave Barry Does Japan**

Alan Booth's **The Roads to Sata** and its sequel, **Looking for the Lost: Journeys Through a Vanishing Japan**

Peter Carey's **Wrong About Japan**

David Chadwick's **Thank You and OK!: An American Zen Failure in Japan**

Cathy Davidson's thoughtful **36 Views of Mount Fiji: On Finding Myself in Japan**

Josie Dew's **A Ride in the Neon Sun**

Bruce Feiler's **Learning to Bow: Inside the Heart of Japan**

Pico Iyer's **The Lady and the Monk: Four Seasons in Kyoto**

Will Ferguson's rollicking **Hokkaido Highway Blues: Hitchhiking Japan**

David Mura's **Turning Japanese**

Donald Keene's **Chronicles of My Life: An American in the Heart of Japan** (fascinating look at the life of a man who brought Japanese studies to the American cultural landscape)

Leila Philip's memoir **The Road Through Miyama**, which tells of her apprenticeship to a master potter in a small Japanese village

Christopher Ross's **Mishima's Sword: Travels in Search of a Samurai Legend**

Kate T. Williamson's **A Year in Japan** (an artist's journal)

JORDAN

There aren't a lot of armchair travel books devoted specifically to Jordan. In fact, aside from a few guidebooks, Jordan is usually lumped in with the rest of the Middle East—you'll find a chapter about it here and there in most books about that region. Or, as seen in the following recommendations, you can pretty easily find a book about the history and art of Jordan. I am, though, still looking for the perfect book that will tell me what the heart of the country is like. Until then, here's what I've discovered and enjoyed.

In **Leap of Faith: Memoirs of an Unexpected Life**, Queen Noor describes her life as both wife and, later, widow of King Hussein of Jordan. Much more than a trophy wife, the queen worked for peace in the Middle East and developed projects to aid the poverty-stricken citizens of her country.

Benjamin Orbach's **Live from Jordan: Letters Home from My Journey Through the Middle East** perhaps came closest to what I was looking for—it's entertaining and enlightening.

Married to a Bedouin by Marguerite van Geldermalsen is the true story of how a young New Zealand nurse met and married a man of the desert, settling down in the city of Petra.

Getty Publications brought out E. Borgia's **Jordan: Past and Present: Petra, Jerash, Amman**, a book that allows western readers to see the beauties of the country at three of its most well-known sites (although, to be honest, I'd heard of only two of them before I discovered this book).

Harry S. Abrams is another publisher specializing in art books. One in their Discoveries series is Christian Auge and Jean-Marie Dentzer's **Petra: Lost City of the Ancient World**; it's certainly useful for the contemporary traveler. While poring over these last two titles, I was remembering a line of a poem by John William Burgon that my mother used to quote about Petra: "a rose-red city, half as old as time."

JUST SO MUCH GREEK TO ME

Although I have studiously stayed away from including guidebooks in *Book Lust To Go*, I couldn't resist recommending Philip Matyszak's **Ancient Athens on 5 Drachmas a Day**, a charming amalgamation of contemporary guide, history, art, and literature—an unbeatable recipe for reading entertainment and information (not to mention an enjoyable trip). And—should your journey take you further afield—don't forget to check out Matyszak's **Ancient Rome on 5 Denarii a Day**.

I think I can guarantee that you'll enjoy **Roumeli: Travels in Northern Greece** and **Mani: Travels in the Southern Peloponnese** by Patrick Leigh Fermor. Together, they are two of the best pure armchair travel books about Greece ever written. Long out of print, they were—I'm thrilled to say—recently reissued by New York Review Books Classics. Not only is Fermor one of the best travel companions you'll ever encounter, he is also able to bring to life the places he goes and the people he meets. He's one of those writers whose frequent digressions from his stated topic only improve the books.

A good novel set in Greece is **Alcestis** by Katharine Beutner. For those of you who aren't up on your Greek mythology, Alcestis is the woman who sacrificed herself to Hermes in the place of her beloved husband.

It was so obvious to me that Zachary Mason had a terrific time creating **The Lost Books of the Odyssey** (that is, beyond the hard work of the actual writing), and you'll have a ball reading these reimaginings of the story of Odysseus. Mason's a brilliant writer; these are witty, serious, and sad—and sometimes all three at the same time.

Other excellent choices include Sara Wheeler's nonfiction account of her travels, **Evia: Travels on an Undiscovered Greek Island** (originally published under the title **An Island Apart: Travels in Evia**); **Eurydice Street: A Place in Athens**, a memoir by Sofka Zinovieff; **Dinner with Persephone: Travels in Greece** by Patricia Storace; **An Island in Greece: On the Shore of Skopelos** by Michael Carroll; and **The Summer of My Greek Taverna: A Memoir** by Tom Stone.

Anne Zouroudi's **The Messenger of Athens** is the first in a series of mysteries; each is based on one of the seven deadly sins. The detective, Hermes Diaktoros, arrives on the island of Thiminos literary history that many people—even the most devoted readers, like me—are unfamiliar with.

If you stopped someone browsing the fiction section of the library or bookstore and asked them to name a Kiwi writer (after first explaining, if need be, what country the nickname refers to), the chances are, if they know of one writer, that writer is most likely going to be Keri Hulme, whose **The Bone People** was a winner of the (then) Booker Prize in 1985. It's one of those books that you either love or hate. It's definitely not an easy book to read, but if you have the inclination and patience, I found it to be a rewarding novel.

Native New Zealander Janet Frame is best known for her three-volume autobiography (and the film made from the second book), consisting of **To the Is-Land**, **An Angel at My Table**, and **The Envoy from Mirror City**, but if that's all you've read, try her novel **Towards Another Summer**. It was published after her death and is filled with a yearning to be home, wherever that may be. Another good novel of hers is **Living in the Maniototo**, which is more lighthearted than some of her other writing. **Prizes: The Selected Stories of Janet Frame** showcases her talents as a short story writer. (I've found the stories are best read slowly, in between other books, and not at one go as if it were a novel.)

Speaking of short stories by New Zealand writers, don't neglect reading Katherine Mansfield's, especially "The Garden Party." It's brilliant.

Other contemporary Kiwi books and writers include Maurice Gee (don't miss his trilogy that begins with **Plumb**, as well as the award-winning **Blindsight**); Patricia Grace, a Maori writer whose books are both beautifully written and very depressing—you might try her Montana New Zealand Book Awards–winning novel, **Tu**; Nigel Cox's **Tarzan Presley**, which takes two universal icons and melds them together (it's very hard to find, but worth the search), or **The Cowboy Dog** (a coming-of-age tale); Maurice Shadbolt's **Season of the Jew** (excellent historical fiction, set in the nineteenth century and based on the life of Te Kooti, a Maori; Rachael King's first novel, **The Sound of Butterflies**; Damien Wilkins's **The Fainter** (and others); and **Here at the End of the World We Learn to Dance** by Lloyd Jones, set in (very) rural New Zealand at the end of World War I, and then, in the present, in Wellington. If you're familiar with this New Zealander's work, it's probably due to the popularity (well earned) of the multi-award-winning **Mister Pip**, which takes place on an unnamed island in the South Seas.

Christina Thompson's memoir **Come On Shore and We Will Kill and Eat You All: A New Zealand Story** weaves her personal experiences (falling in love with and marrying a Maori) with a general overview of the culture clash between westerners and the native Maori tribes.

KOREA—NORTH AND SOUTH

I can't quite believe that many of us are going to head off for a vacation in North Korea any time soon. But who knows? Just in case, here are some books you'll want to read.

Chances are that James Church's atmospheric (rather than fast-moving) novel **A Corpse in the Koryo** is the closest you'll get to North Korea. (After reading it, you'll probably count yourself lucky that it is!) This is the first in a series of mysteries featuring Inspector O of the Pyongyang Police Department. The pseudonymous author spent many years as an intelligence officer in the Far East and clearly knows pretty much all there is to know about North Korean society. Inspector O is smart, pragmatic, and a bit of a romantic—much like Lew Archer, in the Ross MacDonald mysteries, or Arkady Renko, in Martin Cruz Smith's **Gorky Park** and sequels. Church uses details, both small and large (from broken cameras and stolen teakettles to the all-pervasive atmosphere of fear, deprivation, graft, and mistrust that pervades the lives of North Koreans) to make the setting palpably real.

Seoul and surrounding environs in the 1970s is the setting for a series of mysteries by Martin Limón. Military Police Sergeant George Sueño, who, along with his partner Ernie Bascom, normally investigates crimes involving black marketing, drugs, and prostitution among the American troops, narrates them. In their sixth outing, **G. I. Bones**, the crime is a cold case that occurred right after the Korean War ended—twenty years before—and its solution opens windows on Sueño's past that he thought he'd closed forever. Limón offers a clear view into a time and a place that's unfamiliar to many of us. If you like this mystery, try my other favorite: **The Wandering Ghost**.

Another terrific mystery—this one set primarily in North Korea—is Gus Lee's oldie but goodie, **Tiger's Tail**.

If you were to pick a locale in which to set a novel, I don't think you could find anyplace more remarkable than the setting of Jeff Talarigo's **The Ginseng Hunter**. It takes place along the Tumen

River, which divides China from Korea. The themes—love, war, political oppression, the grief of solitude, the solitude of grief—all make this an unforgettable reading experience.

In **Korea, A Walk Through the Land of Miracles**, Simon Winchester provides probably the friendliest guide to South Korea, describing, with his usual panache, its history, geography, and culture.

The best book for the nonhistorian on the Korean War (which was not, in actuality, ever declared a war, but rather described as a "police action") is David Halberstam's **The Coldest Winter: America and the Korean War**. It's long, thorough, not tedious, and filled with fascinating and little-known facts.

The sections of Chang-rae Lee's brilliant fourth novel **The Surrendered** that are set in Korea (and Manchuria) during the "police action" make excruciating reading. I can't imagine the pain it must have caused Lee to write them. But oh my goodness, what a splendid novel this is.

In a first novel based on the life of her mother, Eugenia Kim's **The Calligrapher's Daughter** tells a tale of a country and a woman trying to balance the old ways with the new.

All the stories in **Once the Shore** by Paul Yoon are set on a South Korean island; their time frame covers the half-century between just before the Korean War to the present.

The stories of men and women who managed to leave the country form the basis of Barbara Demick's consistently interesting **Nothing to Envy: Ordinary Lives in North Korea**. One of the first things you'll want to do, I suspect, is mull over how ironic the title is.

LAOS

Although there are many books on Indochina or Southeast Asia that include Laos, here are some that focus on the country itself.

Mystery fans rejoice—don't miss these little-known treasures: Colin Cotterill's series starring Dr. Siri Paiboun, coroner to the nation. I'd read these in order: **The Coroner's Lunch, Thirty-Three Teeth, Disco for the Departed, Anarchy and Old Dogs, Curse of the Pogo Stick, The Merry Misogynist,** and **Love Songs from a Shallow Grave**.

In **Lost Over Laos: A True Story of Tragedy, Mystery, and Friendship,** Richard Pyle describes a search for the remains of four combat journalists who were killed in 1971, as the Vietnam War was raging. Horst Faas's photographs complement the tale.

Kao Kalia Yang's affecting memoir, **The Latehomecomer: A Hmong Family Memoir,** remained with me long after I turned over the last page.

LAS VEGAS

For many people (members of my own family among them), Las Vegas is a vacation spot of choice. When it came time to write this section I decided, for some reason that makes total sense to me—maybe because Las Vegas seems to change radically moment by moment and certainly year-by-year—to arrange the recommended titles roughly in order of publication date.

John D. MacDonald is best known for his Travis McGee mysteries (all set in or near Fort Lauderdale, Florida), but his non-series novel **The Only Girl in the Game** is like a snapshot of Las Vegas circa 1960; it's so well plotted and the portrait of Las Vegas is so well drawn that reading it is like taking a trip back in time.

Fear and Loathing in Las Vegas: A Savage Journey to the Heart of the American Dream by Hunter S. Thompson is a drug-hazy account of adventures in the city that first appeared in *Rolling Stone* in 1971, and set the tone for the stoned decade to come.

Although I'm generally not a true crime fan, I did quite enjoy these two books: James McManus's **Positively Fifth Street: Murderers, Cheetahs, and Binion's World Series of Poker** and Nicholas Pileggi's **Casino: Love and Honor in Las Vegas**, an account of the two men who ran the Mob (and therefore ran Las Vegas) in the 1980s. In addition to being both enlightening and nicely written, Pileggi's book is a good companion read for McDonald's novel.

In **Beautiful Children** Charles Bock, a native of the city, portrays the dark underside of Las Vegas through the experiences of a twelve-year-old boy who leaves his home in the suburbs and disappears into the maw of glitter and grief of Sin City. And the sins are major, though not those that you might first expect.

And fans of Carl Hiaassen's and Donald Westlake's capers will enjoy Chris Ewan's novels that take place in different cities around the world—**The Good Thief's Guide to Vegas** is the third in the series, but there's no need to read them in any particular order. Charlie Howard, the eponymous hero, also appears in **The Good**

Thief's Guide to Amsterdam and The Good Thief's Guide
to Paris.

LEAVENED IN LEBANON

If Lebanon's your destination, don't miss these.
Waltz with Bashir: A Lebanon War Story is a graphic
novel based on the film of the same name, written and drawn
by Ari Folman and David Polonsky. It's about the experiences of an
Israeli soldier during the 1982 attacks on Shatila and Sabra.

Novels either set in Lebanon or by Lebanese writers include
Beaufort by Ron Leshem (about an Israeli based in southern
Lebanon whose commando team is undergoing constant attack
by Hezbollah); Nathalie Abi-Ezzi's **A Girl Made of Dust**, set in a
small town just outside Beirut; Rawi Hage's **De Niro's Game**; and
The Hakawati, in which Rabih Alameddine weaves the whole
history of the Middle East into the story of one unforgettable
Lebanese family (this is not a book to rush through—you have to
take the time to savor what Alameddine has accomplished). If you
appreciate Alameddine's style and substance, you might also enjoy
his novels **Koolaids: The Art of War** and **I, the Divine: A Novel
in First Chapters**.

All of Hanan al-Shaykh's novels deal with the role of women in
the Middle East, particularly in her native Lebanon. Her best known
is probably **Women of Sand and Myrrh**, so I'd start there; I can
also highly recommend her epistolary novel, **Beirut Blues**.

Al-Shaykh also wrote **The Locust and the Bird: My Mother's
Story** as a way of coming to understand just what it took for

her mother to divorce her father in a society where women were expected to accept what fate dealt them and any deviation from that behavior was severely punished.

Other nonfiction not to miss includes Joel Chasnoff's **The 188th Crybaby Brigade: A Skinny Jewish Kid from Chicago Fights Hezbollah: A Memoir**, in which an Ivy League–educated comedian whose career is going nowhere decides to change directions, joins the Israeli Defense Forces, and is sent to Lebanon (hard to believe this could be funny, but it is); **Origins: A Memoir** by Amin Maalouf includes not only his family's history, but also the amazing story of his grandfather's trip to Havana to bring his younger brother home; and Vénus Khoury-Ghata's **A House at the Edge of Tears**.

There's a full chapter about the refugee camps in Lebanon in Caroline Moorehead's devastating **Human Cargo: A Journey Among Refugees**, and one of the most thought-provoking books I've read in years is Fouad Ajami's cultural history of the Middle East in **The Dream Palace of the Arabs: A Generation's Odyssey**.

LIBERIA

The House at Sugar Beach: In Search of a Lost African Childhood** by Helene Cooper, who formerly worked for the *Wall Street Journal* and is now diplomatic correspondent for the *New York Times*, describes her idyllic childhood and the horrors following the descent of Liberia into civil war.

The Darling by Russell Banks is the story of Hannah Musgrave, American born and bred, a child of hopeful dreams and political protest, who flees the FBI's clutches and moves to Liberia in 1976, where she marries one of the rising stars of the growing revolutionary movement there. Now living in relative seclusion on a farm in upstate New York, she travels back to that war-torn country to find her three sons. Banks's novel features a heroine whom you can't entirely embrace in friendship and good will, but whose idealism and good faith you can't deny.

Political junkies won't want to miss Ellen Johnson Sirleaf's memoir **This Child Will Be Great**. It's the remarkable story of a little girl growing up in the 1930s and '40s in a dilapidated area of Monrovia, the country's capital, and ending up in 2006 with her election as Liberia's (and Africa's) first woman president.

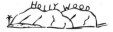

LOS ANGELES: CITY OF ANGELS

Genre readers are really in luck when it comes to L.A.—some of the best-known writers of the past and present set their books there.

From the past, there's James Cain (**Mildred Pierce** is the one to pick up first) and Joseph Wambaugh (especially **The Choirboys**; the title is totally ironic, but you have to read the book to find out why). Wambaugh's nonfiction work, **The Onion Field**, is one of the few true crime books that I've really enjoyed. It takes place in L.A. in 1963, recounting the events that occur after two policemen pull over a car for a routine traffic stop.

From the present there's Walter Moseley, whose Easy Rawlins novels, read in order, present a history of the city's racial politics. Begin with **Devil in a Blue Dress**, which introduces all the major themes that Mosley explores throughout the series.

Other favorites of mine include Michael Connelly (especially his very early novels, including **The Black Echo**, **The Black Ice**, and **The Concrete Blond**) and Robert Crais (especially **The Watchman**, featuring Joe Pike).

For a look at cool L.A., try the lighthearted mysteries by Harley Jane Kozak and Susan Kandel. Kozak's main character is Wollie (short for Wollstonecraft) Shelley, a greeting-card designer whose antics will delight you. Some of my favorite parts of **Dating Dead Men** and her other novels are the zany characters who populate Wollie's life. Kandel's character, Cece Caruso, writes biographies about famous mystery writers (and thus always stumbles across a body or two in her researches). Although it's not necessary to read them in order, the first one is **I Dreamed I Married Perry Mason**; my favorite happens to be **Christietown: A Novel About Vintage Clothing, Romance, Mystery, and Agatha Christie**. Fans of Janet Evanovich's New Jersey romps will enjoy these West Coast read-alikes.

But there are lots of terrific non-genre novels (old and new) about the City of Angels, including **The Tortilla Curtain** by T. C. Boyle; Bebe Moore Campbell's **Brothers and Sisters**; Marisa Silver's **Babe in Paradise**; Michael Tolkin's **The Player**; **The Day of the Locust** by Nathanael West; **Crescent** by Diana Abu-Jaber; and **Play It As It Lays** by Joan Didion.

And nonfiction as well: Sandra Tsing Loh's **Depth Takes a Holiday: Essays from Lesser Los Angeles**, and **Cadillac Desert: The American West and Its Disappearing Water** by Marc Reisner (which broadens the geographical narrowness of this section considerably), for two.

If you're looking for topnotch nonfiction writing about the state (not just L.A. or San Francisco), take a look at John McPhee's **Assembling California**, the last book in his Annals of the Former World series. If anyone can make geology both essential reading and understandable by the interested layperson, it's McPhee. A friend once mentioned to me that even though he's read McPhee's essays in *The New Yorker*, he's always drawn to reread them in book form because McPhee's style is so captivating.

LYME REGIS

If you're going to Lyme Regis, a wonderfully broody and very atmospheric city in England that seems to be on the verge of falling into the ocean, the book to turn to first is **The French Lieutenant's Woman** by John Fowles. Read it for how Fowles fills the story with Lyme (and, if the book is new to you, for the wonderful way he plays with the idea of story itself). If you do travel to this city, you can find The Cobb and the rock formation known as Granny's Teeth that Fowles refers to in his novel.

Another novel to pick up is Jane Austen's **Persuasion**. Here Anne and others stroll the windy streets of Lyme and silly Louisa Musgrove jumps from The Cobb as she flirts with Captain Wentworth.

Remarkable Creatures by Tracy Chevalier is a Victorian-era novel focusing on real women—Mary Anning and Elizabeth Philpot—who were speculating about evolution and the nature of the world before Darwin; together they changed history (though they got little credit for it).

Note for mystery fans: There's even a terrific Colin Dexter mystery called **The Way Through the Woods**, in which Inspector Morse, whom we usually find operating out of Oxford, travels to Lyme Regis on vacation and stumbles on a crime involving a missing Swedish woman who disappeared while on holiday there.

THE MAINE CHANCE

People go to Maine for the beauty of its coastline, the romance of its forests, the fun of clamming, and the coziness of its small towns. There are many great reads set in the Pine Tree State. Here are my favorites.

One of the classics that has kept its charm is Sarah Orne Jewett's **The Country of the Pointed Firs**, originally published in 1896. It's set in a coastal village and is marked by the acuity of its observations, its appreciation for nature, and its gentle insights into the lives of women. (In a strange way, it reminded me of Elizabeth Gaskell's **Cranford**, although the two books have really nothing in common except that they're word pictures of a particular time and place.)

All three of Elizabeth Strout's novels are set in Maine. There's **Amy and Isabelle** (one of the male characters is a contender for the most loathsome man in fiction, second only to Humbert Humbert, in my opinion); **Abide with Me**, which takes place in 1959 (fans of Marilynne Robinson's **Gilead** and **Home** will probably enjoy it very much); and **Olive Kitteridge**, a collection of linked short stories that won the Pulitzer Prize. Book groups take note: all of these would make an excellent choice for discussion.

Before she became famous for **Eat, Pray, Love**, Elizabeth Gilbert wrote a terrific novel called **Stern Men**, which is set on an island twenty miles north of the coast of Maine. Fort Niles is separated from another island only by a small channel, but each island's inhabitants, mostly lobstermen and their families, loathe anyone from the other island. After attending boarding school out of state, Ruth returns to Fort Niles determined to end the internecine warring—partly by falling in love with the "wrong" young man.

When you finish the Gilbert novel, take a look at these two reader-friendly micro-histories of the lobster industry: **The Lobster Coast: Rebels, Rusticators, and the Struggle for a Forgotten Frontier** by Colin Woodard and **The Secret Life of Lobsters: How Fishermen and Scientists Are Unraveling the Mysteries of Our Favorite Crustacean** by Trevor Corson. Corson is a marine biologist and a third-generation lobsterman—here he describes what's known, and not, about the lobster, and intersperses that with stories of his family's life on Little Cranberry Island, Maine.

I frequently suggest Stephen King's **Lisey's Story** to readers who believe books in the horror genre are too, well, horrible for them. It takes place primarily in a non-supernatural Maine and is quite a good choice for book groups, as well.

Some Maine-based classics include Louise Dickinson Rich's **We Took to the Woods**; Henry David Thoreau's **The Maine Woods**; and **Arundel** by Kenneth Roberts, which recounts Benedict

Arnold's march to Quebec as told by Steven Nason, a (fictional) young man from Arundel, Maine. (Nearly every high school student in the state has read this book.)

One book that should become a classic is Bernd Heinrich's **A Year in the Maine Woods**, in which he describes the time he spent in a small cabin deep in the trees pretty much alone except for his pet raven, Jack. When I finished this, I wanted to spend a year in the Maine woods, too, seeing, hearing, experiencing, and knowing all that Heinrich did. And, of course, to get a raven of my own named Jack.

Contemporary Maine novels include the Tinker Cove mysteries of Leslie Meier (there are lots of them, so if you enjoy them you're in real luck; there's no need to start with the first one); the bed-and-breakfast-themed mysteries of Karen MacInerney, especially **Murder Most Maine**; and Paul Doiron's first—but I hope not last—mystery, **The Poacher's Son**. Doiron is editor-in-chief of *Down East: The Magazine of Maine*, and he knows the state well.

And please don't forget Cathie Pelletier's funny and poignant novels; their characters still shine in my memory. **The Bubble Reputation** and **The Funeral Makers** (among others) will definitely give you a feeling for the quirky charms of the state.

MAKING TRACKS BY TRAIN

I seem to be quoting Edna St. Vincent Millay often these days; there's a poem of hers called "Travel" that I memorized years ago because it has always described how I wish I felt—especially the last verse, which ends: "Yet there isn't a train I wouldn't take, / No matter where it's going."

I've always wanted to be the kind of person whose adventurous nature would lead me to emulate the poem's speaker and just take a train ride for the joy of it. My longtime dream—sadly unlikely to be realized at this point in my life—is to travel from Sydney, Australia, across the enormous country to Perth by train. I constantly console myself by seeking out and compulsively reading the accounts of other, more adventuresome travelers. It's a shame that there aren't more contemporary writings about train rides available to the armchair traveler, but we're so lucky to have the ones we do.

In **The Big Red Train Ride**, über-traveler Eric Newby, along with his long-suffering and mostly very patient wife, Wanda, traveled from Moscow on a three-thousand-mile journey to the Soviet Far East and the Sea of Japan in 1977. The description of their trip—written in Newby's always understated humor—is a delight, although you might be grateful (as I was) to be reading it in a warm house, wearing flannel pajamas, and having cups and cups of hot tea readily to hand.

Paul Theroux is a connoisseur of long train rides as well. Many of his books are about train travel—the various trains he's taken, the people he's met along the way, and the experiences that ensued. My favorite is **The Great Railway Bazaar: By Train Through Asia**, but others include **The Old Patagonian Express: By Train Through the Americas**; **Riding the Iron Rooster: By Train Through China**; and **Ghost Train to the Eastern Star: On the Tracks of** *The Great Railway Bazaar*, which retraces his 1975 journey.

Andrew Eames's **The 8:55 to Baghdad** not only describes his 2002 train journey from London to Iraq, but also offers a look back at the life of mystery writer Agatha Christie, who took the Orient Express on the same three-thousand-mile journey in 1928. (Fans of Christie's book **Murder on the Orient Express** will find much to explain its genesis here.) Eames is a delightful travel companion— well read, personable, able to remain calm in the face of calamity, and willing to overlook rude behavior and bad food. He revels, as all real travelers seem to, in good company and interesting scenery.

The Selected Works of T. S. Spivet by Reif Larsen is a winsome novel about a young boy traveling from Wyoming to Washington, D.C., by himself, by train. (There's a bit more about the book in the section "WY Ever Not?")

Other books that will make you seek out any long-distance train journey still available include these:

> Jenny Diski's **Stranger on a Train: Daydreaming and Smoking Around America with Interruptions**
> Henry Kisor's **Zephyr: Tracking a Dream Across America**

Terry Pindell's **Yesterday's Train: A Rail Odyssey Through Mexican History**; **Making Tracks: An American Rail Odyssey**; and **Last Train to Toronto: A Canadian Rail Odyssey**

William T. Vollmann's **Riding Toward Everywhere**

And, of course, the following classic crime novels:

Agatha Christie's **Murder on the Orient Express** and **The Mystery of the Blue Train**, and Graham Greene's **Orient Express**

MALAYSIA

Just to offer a little background: Malaysia is a country in Southeast Asia. Thailand is to its north, the South China Sea is to its east, and the Strait of Malacca is to its west, with the separate country of Singapore at Malaysia's very southern tip. It's composed of thirteen states: Johore, Kedah, Kelantan, Melaka (formerly Malacca), Negeri Sembilan, Pahang, Penang, Perak, Perlis, Sabah, Sarawak, Selangor, and Terengganu. Its capital city, Kuala Lumpur, and the island of Labuan are separate federal territories. Malaysia was established in September 1963. Whew.

It's always good to get in at the beginning of the series, especially if it's as promising as Shamini Flint's **Inspector Singh Investigates: A Most Peculiar Malaysian Murder**. Traveling from his home in Singapore to KL (as Kuala Lumpur is called by those in the know) Singh must try to extricate a former model from death row for the murder of her ex-husband—a crime he's sure she didn't commit, although all the signs point to her guilt and the Malaysian police aren't budging in their belief that their case against her is airtight.

The cartoonist (or graphic novelist) Lat is beloved in his native Malaysia. Some of his books are finally becoming available here. I read the first one, **Kampung Boy**, which is the story of his early years, and—surprisingly—I think I learned more about the country and its people from this graphic memoir than from almost anything else that I've read about the country.

Other books with a Malaysian setting include Shirley Geok-lin Lim's **Joss and Gold** and **Among the White Moon Faces: An Asian-American Memoir of Homelands**; as well as **The Consul's File** by Paul Theroux, a series of connected short stories that take place in the 1970s.

MARTHA'S VINEYARD

Martha's Vineyard is an island in Massachusetts off of Cape Cod. It's studded by the summer homes of many famous people, including the Kennedys. I've never been but am quite open to invitations to visit!

David Kinney's lively **The Big One: An Island, an Obsession, and the Furious Pursuit of a Great Fish** is an in-depth account of the annual thirty-five-day Striped Bass and Bluefish Derby, a contest that takes place after the summer tourists have gone home; it pits teenagers against recovering alcoholics against hedge fund managers and charter boat captains out for a (long) busman's holiday.

Jill Nelson's **Finding Martha's Vineyard: African Americans at Home on an Island** explores one of the most interesting aspects of that bucolic place: for centuries African Americans have lived there, in their own enclaves, either for a summer getaway or year round. In addition to her own memories of the importance of Oak Bluffs in her life, Nelson includes reminiscences from author and law professor Stephen Carter, film director Spike Lee, novelist Bebe Moore Campbell, and others.

In **On the Vineyard: A Year in the Life of an Island**, Jane Carpineto describes the varied people and places she encounters during her sojourn there.

Birders will both adore and mourn over the changes that have occurred since E. Vernon Laux wrote **Bird News: Vagrants and Visitors on a Peculiar Island** a relatively short eleven years ago, in 1999. It's enough to make you want to travel back in time . . .

Philip R. Craig wrote nineteen mysteries set on Martha's Vineyard, beginning with 1991's **A Beautiful Place to Die**. His detective is Vietnam veteran, former cop, chef, and fisherman Jeff Jackson.

Other novels set on Martha's Vineyard include Anne Rivers Siddons's **Up Island**; **Illumination Night** by Alice Hoffman; and Dorothy West's **The Wedding**, which is set among an African American community much like the one Jill Nelson describes. (Indeed, West is one of the writers who contributed to Nelson's book.)

A MENTION OF THE MIDDLE EAST

As we all know from our newspaper reading, tensions in the Middle East seem never-ending. The history of the region is complex, emotions run high, and even choosing particular words when writing about the area is fraught with ambiguities. There are a great many titles to choose from, so without regard to fear or favor, I offer a list of books that are all certain to broaden your knowledge, increase your understanding of this part of the world, and be enjoyable (if sometimes uncomfortable) reads.

> Susan Abulhawa's **Mornings in Jenin: A Novel**
>
> Rich Cohen's illuminating and provocative **Israel Is Real** gave me much to think about.
>
> Larry Collins and Dominique Lapierre's **O Jerusalem!: Day by Day and Minute by Minute: The Historic Struggle for Jerusalem and the Birth of Israel**
>
> Alexandra Hobbet's **Small Kingdoms** gives us a detailed and intimate word picture of the life of a Kuwaiti family in the period between the two Gulf Wars.
>
> David Ignatius's **Agents of Innocence** (spy novel aficionados should definitely seek it out)
>
> Jim Krane's **City of Gold: Dubai and the Dream of Capitalism**
>
> Maliha Masood's **Zaatar Days, Henna Nights: Adventures, Dreams, and Destinations Across the Middle East**
>
> Amos Oz's **A Tale of Love and Darkness** gives a gorgeous account of his life and that of his parents, who came to Palestine from Lithuania in the 1930s.
>
> Hugh Pope's **Dining with Al-Qaeda** is a culmination of all that he's learned and experienced during thirty years of travel throughout the Middle East, beginning

Mrs. Bliss dislikes schmutz intensely); Helen Yglesias's **The Girls**; and Ana Veciana-Suarez's **The Chin Kiss King**.

Nonfiction about the area abounds as well:

Journalist Ann Louise Bardach's **Cuba Confidential: Love and Vengeance in Miami and Havana** (detailing the complicated relationship between the two cities); Joan Didion's **Miami** (it has the same gorgeous writing as all her other books); Edna Buchanan's **The Corpse Had a Familiar Face**; Joann Biondi's **Miami Beach Memories: A Nostalgic Chronicle of Days Gone By**; **We Own This Game: A Season in the Adult World of Youth Football** by Robert Andrew Powell (ever wonder why the Florida college teams are so consistently ranked at the top of the charts? This book helps answer why that's so.); **Last Train to Paradise: Henry Flagler and the Spectacular Rise and Fall of the Railroad That Crossed an Ocean** by Florida native Les Standiford, who also wrote a bunch of suspense novels about Miami contractor John Deal; and Ann Armbruster's **The Life and Times of Miami Beach**.

NAPLES

As a child, one of the most traumatic events of my reading life was discovering a book in the library about the death of a boy and his dog as a result of the eruption of Mount Vesuvius in 79 B.C.E. It may have been based on Louis Untermeyer's short story "The Dog of Pompeii," but since I was too traumatized to have ever gone back to look for or at it, I can't be sure. In any case, the idea of nature going ballistic (to mix a metaphor) and burying two towns beneath tons of ash has remained in a not-so-little corner of my mind. Not to mention all the other bits of information regarding the event that have seeped into my consciousness since—one being that Pliny the Elder refused to leave the area, as he was determined to garner every bit of scientific information that he could from the impending disaster. He died there. Which is all to explain why I—deliberately or unconsciously—have simply avoided reading books set in that part of Italy.

Avoided, that is, until I discovered prize-winning Australian novelist Shirley Hazzard (don't miss her novels **The Transit of Venus** and **The Great Fire**). She fell in love with Naples, Italy, when she first arrived there in 1956 to work for the United Nations, at a time when the city was still marked by the bombings it took during World War II. Despite the time Hazzard spent in cities great and small around the world, Naples retained its central place in her heart. She wrote about it often; these brief essays are collected in a lovely little book, **The Ancient Shore**. The book also includes a long essay written for *The New Yorker* by her husband, scholar and writer Francis Steegmuller, about a traumatic occurrence in Naples that well describes both the best and worst of this chaotic and beautiful city situated in the shadow of Mount Vesuvius.

In Robert Harris's **Pompeii**, set in the days leading up to the volcano's great eruption, the author mixes heart-stopping suspense with fascinating tidbits of information about first-century life in the Roman Empire, with the result that this novel should please those looking for a classic thriller as well as fans of historical fiction.

Other grand novels set in Naples include these:

Shirley Hazzard's early and most likely autobiographical novel **The Bay of Noon** is about a young woman coming to Naples to start a new life but finding it difficult to rid herself of the old one. It was originally published in 1970 but reissued in 2003.

Not only is Sir William Hamilton, the British ambassador to the Kingdom of Two Sicilies (of which Naples was once a part), in love with volcanoes, he also falls rather desperately in love with, and marries, the beautiful Emma Lyon, his nephew's mistress, who in turn falls in love (desperately) with Lord Horatio Nelson, Britain's greatest naval hero. I'm exhausted just describing the plot. **The Volcano Lover** is historical romance for intellectuals, as you would no doubt expect from its author, iconic intellectual Susan Sontag.

NEBRASKA: THE BIG EMPTY

Except for the Cornhuskers football team, whom I loyally despised all the time I lived in Oklahoma, and Willa Cather's **My Ántonia**, I never thought much about the state until I started reading some really wonderful books—both fiction and nonfiction—about it. And here they are.

Pamela Carter Joern's writes exquisite works of fiction, including **The Plain Sense of Things** and **The Floor of the Sky**.

Ron Hansen's **Nebraska: Stories** are terrific examples of a writer who can't seem to write a bad sentence—not that I'd ever want him to, of course. The subjects here range from the past to the present, and each is worth a slow, intent reading.

Tom McNeal's first novel, **Goodnight, Nebraska**, tells the story of a young man trying to find himself in a world that's not often forgiving.

Ladette Randolph and Nina Shevchuk-Murray edited **The Big Empty: Contemporary Nebraska Nonfiction Writers**, a collection of essays (and some excerpts) that offers a diverse look at people's lives in the state at various times and under various conditions. Writers include both the well known (Ted Kooser and Ron Hansen) and those unfamiliar to most readers (Michael Anania, Delphine Red Shirt, and William Kloefkorn).

Polly Spence's **Moving Out: A Nebraska Woman's Life** is an amazingly unsentimental memoir of growing up in a small Nebraska town.

Roger Welsch's **My Nebraska: The Good, the Bad, and the Husker** is a humorous love letter to his home state.

Other books set in Nebraska, or by Nebraska authors, include Stephanie Kallos's lovely **Sing Them Home**, which takes place in a small Welsh community there; Ann Patchett's **The Magician's Assistant**; Jim Harrison's **Dalva** and **The Road Home**, which continues the tale (once you meet Dalva, it's nearly impossible to forget her—she's that fully formed as a character. I still think these are Harrison's best books.); George Shaffner's **In the Land of Second Chances** (and all his other novels set in Ebb, Nebraska); **The Echo Maker** by Richard Powers (one of the author's most brilliant and thought-provoking novels); and Timothy Schaffert's **Devils in the Sugar Shop** (funny, raunchy, set in Omaha, and peopled by the participants in an erotic writing workshop).

at www.seattlechannel.org/videos/video
.asp?ID=3030901.)

Will Eisner's **New York: Life in the Big City** includes four of the cartoonist's graphic books: **New York, The Building, City People Notebook,** and **Invisible People**

Pete Hamill's **Downtown: My Manhattan**

Mark Helprin's great novel, **Winter's Tale**

Adam Langer's tale of Manhattan real estate, **Ellington Boulevard: A Novel in A-Flat**

Phillip Lopate's **Waterfront: A Walk Around Manhattan** and (as editor) **Writing New York: A Literary Anthology**, which includes both poetry and prose (fiction and nonfiction) about the city, written by a deliriously diverse mix of writers, including Sara Teasdale, Edgar Allan Poe, Langston Hughes, Jane Jacobs, William Burroughs, Dawn Powell, Lincoln Steffens, and Oscar Hijuelos. It's much too bulky a tome to carry around with you, but perfect for getting into the spirit of Manhattan before you go.

Cheryl Mendelson's **Morningside Heights** and sequels

Jan Morris's **Manhattan '45**

New York Stories: Landmark Writing from Four Decades of *New York* **Magazine**

The New York Times **Book of New York: 549 Stories of the People, the Events, and the Life of the City—Past and Present**

Eric Sanderson's **Mannahatta: A Natural History of New York City**, with a fabulous assortment of illustrations by Markley Boyer, is too big to carry around, sadly, but is so interesting to browse through at home.

Russell Shorto's detailed **The Island at the Center of the World: The Epic Story of Dutch Manhattan and the Forgotten Colony That Shaped America**

NEWFOUNDLAND

I can't imagine taking a trip to Newfoundland without reading Annie Proulx's **The Shipping News** and Howard Norman's **The Bird Artist**; both grace my own bookshelves. Try the books that follow as well.

Lisa Moore's **February** is a fabulous novel that tells—in bewitchingly beautiful prose—the story of a woman left widowed by the historically violent storm on February 14, 1982, that killed all eighty-four crew members of the oil rig *Ocean Ranger*. Another of her novels set in Newfoundland is **Alligator**.

And these works of nonfiction:

All the time I was reading Robert Finch's **The Iambics of Newfoundland: Notes from an Unknown Shore** I kept wishing I could have followed in Finch's footsteps as he made his way—over a number of years—across the landscape of one of Canada's most unusual provinces. What a lovely tribute to the flora and fauna (two- and four-legged), history, and culture of Newfoundland.

Farley Mowat is one of Canada's best-known writers and conservationists. His books range from humorous (**The Dog Who Wouldn't Be**, which is set on the prairies of Saskatchewan) to more serious titles like his memoir **Bay of Spirits**, which not only describes how he met his wife, Claire, while traveling on a tramp steamer around the coast of Newfoundland, but also provides a picture of the people who live and work in the (much depleted) fishing industry. A good companion read for this book is Mark Kurlansky's **Cod: A Biography of the Fish That Changed the World**.

NEWS FROM N'ORLEANS

Many, but not all, of the newer books on the city have to do with Hurricane Katrina and its aftermath. Here are my favorites.

Tim Gautreaux takes us back to New Orleans in the years following World War I in **The Missing**, a novel I discovered at a time when I was despairing about ever finding anything good to read again. I find it odd but accurate to describe Gautreaux's writing style as both spare and lyrical. But it is. When three-year-old Lily is kidnapped in the New Orleans department store where Sam Simoneaux works as an in-house detective, he makes it his mission to locate her. Much of the novel takes place on a riverboat—a four-deck, 300-foot stern-wheeler where Lily's parents work as musicians. The novel moves as you might imagine the Mississippi itself does, slow, stately, and steady. You may have to consciously slow down to read it (I did)—much as you do with a nineteenth-century novel. All of our senses—smell, taste, sight, and sound—are engaged as we as we slowly turn the pages.

Dave Eggers's **Zeitoun** is a biography-as-novel of Abdulrahman Zeitoun, a New Orleans contractor born in Syria, who decides to send his wife and children out of the city as Hurricane Katrina approaches, but chooses to stay behind himself and ride out the storm. As a result of that decision, he's caught up in a bureaucratic nightmare growing out of the flaws in crisis management and the domestic war on terror.

Other excellent choices include these:

Amanda Boyden's **Babylon Rolling**, featuring a large cast of exquisitely drawn characters who face up to the imminent threat of Hurricane Ivan in 2004.

In **Nine Lives: Death and Life in New Orleans** Dan Baum, a writer for *The New Yorker*, brackets his story of the city and its residents by two classic storms: Hurricane Betsy in 1965 and Katrina in 2005. Through Baum's descriptions, the people he profiles and their lives become intensely important to us.

An excellently readable nonfiction account of Katrina—putting it into historical context—is Douglas Brinkley's **The Great Deluge: Hurricane Katrina, New Orleans, and the Mississippi Gulf Coast**.

Other books set in Nigeria include **I Do Not Come to You by Chance** by Adaobi Tricia Nwaubani, a humorous yet thought-provoking novel about Internet scammers in Nigeria; and Sefi Atta's dynamic first novel, **Everything Good Will Come**, a bitingly funny take on two women's attempts to figure out their roles in post-colonial Lagos.

An important part of the heart-tugging (but not sentimental) and unforgettable novel **Little Bee** by Chris Cleave is set in Nigeria. It's the story of the relationship between an older British woman and a young Nigerian girl whom she and her husband meet on a beach during what is supposed to be an idyllic vacation for the British couple. This is an absolutely perfect choice for book groups.

NORTH AFRICAN NOTES

North Africa is that part of the world that is on the southern edge of the Mediterranean Sea, reaching from Egypt in the east to Tangier in the west. The best book covering the whole area that I've found is Michael Mewshaw's **Between Terror and Tourism: An Overland Journey Across North Africa**. Not only is the first half of the title pretty neat, but since this inviting, chatty account is filled with fascinating bits of information and references to and quotations from other writers (Cavafy and Baudelaire, to name only two), I had to keep putting down the book and copying passages into the notebook I keep for such things. Books on Egypt, a major player in North Africa, can be found in its own self-titled section.

Algeria

Two important works of nonfiction on the history of Algeria and its long, awful fight to free itself from its colonial master, France, are Alistair Horne's **A Savage War of Peace: Algeria 1954–1962** and Ted Morgan's **My Battle of Algiers: A Memoir**.

Elizabeth Hawes's **Camus: A Romance** combines biography (of French writer Albert Camus) with memoir. (Hawes became entranced with Camus when she was a college student.). Although there's much here that takes place in France, there's enough focus on Algiers (and, in particular, Camus's childhood) to make it a necessary accompaniment to any reading for travel-to-Algeria purposes. Or just for the pleasure of encountering a man who had a fine mind and a noble spirit.

Although it was published posthumously and is not considered to be his best novel, Camus's **The First Man** is probably his most autobiographical, and is certainly the one most closely linked to his childhood in Algiers. (Camus was born in Oran, where he set his novels **The Plague** and **The Stranger**.)

Next to Camus, Yasmina Khadra is probably Algeria's most famous writer, although most of his novels are set elsewhere (his best-known novel for American audiences is **The Swallows of Kabul**). The author, who was once a high-ranking military officer with the Algerian army, wrote his books under a (female) pseudonym in order to avoid political repercussions. (He's now in exile, in France.) Mystery lovers on their way to Algeria will want to try Khadra's Inspector Llob series; the first one is **Morituri**, but my favorite is **Double Blank**.

Loving Graham Greene, Gloria Emerson's first novel, is both tragic and funny. Wealthy and eccentric Molly Benson, who has a passion for Graham Greene and his work, travels to Algeria in 1992 (the year after Greene's death) with two friends in order to give money to writers there who are targets of the country's fundamentalists. This is a tale of three innocents abroad, the sort of people who believe that their good works (and pure motives) will protect them from harm. One could easily imagine how much Greene himself would have enjoyed reading it.

Harbor, a wrenching first novel by journalist Lorraine Adams, is about a Muslim from Algeria who arrives illegally in America in the 1990s. Aziz Arkoun is a deserter from the Algerian army and becomes caught up in America's domestic war on terror following 9/11. This is one of those novels that raises uncomfortable questions for readers: how do we know whom to trust; how can we best accommodate new immigrants who are fleeing for their lives but don't qualify as "political refugees" under the law; which should prevail when individual rights come into conflict with what we're told is our national interest; and who or what defines a "terrorist"?

Other novels set in Algeria include Brian Moore's **The Magician's Wife**, which takes place during the Napoleonic period, and Claire Messud's **The Last Life**, which describes the experiences of one French family during the last days of French rule.

For a change of pace, take a look at Joann Sfar's **The Rabbi's Cat** and its sequel, **The Rabbi's Cat 2**, a pair of graphic novels set in the once flourishing Jewish community in Algeria. They're about a cat who swallows a parrot, learns to talk, and develops a devouring (sorry!) interest in everything related to Judaism.

Morocco

Whenever there's talk about literature and Morocco, or travel and Morocco, it's pretty certain that Paul Bowles's life and books will be mentioned early in the conversation, since he spent many years as an expatriate there and is closely identified (at least in American minds) with the country. (See the section "The Sahara: Sand Between Your Toes" for more about Bowles's best-known book.) So try to get whatever you know about the country, and Bowles, out of your head for a while, and concentrate on these.

One of my favorite writers, Edith Wharton, visited the country in 1917 and wrote **In Morocco** about her time there. What took away from the delight of reading a previously unknown—to me— Wharton book was the anti-Semitism that creeps in a bit here and there throughout the text.

Tony Ardizzone's **Larabi's Ox: Stories of Morocco** is a series of interconnected stories about three Americans who arrive in the country for different reasons and find (or not) what they came for.

French Moroccan Tahar Ben Jelloun explores the post-colonial country in **The Last Friend**, the story of the relationship between Ali and Mamed, childhood best friends, now irrevocably separated. The translation by Linda Coverdale is superb, and the story illuminates both the nature of friendship and the state of the country. If you're in the mood for a difficult and soul-destroying read, also try his **This Blinding Absence of Light**.

Other books with a Moroccan setting—or close connection—include Laila Lalami's **Hope and Other Dangerous Pursuits** and **Secret Son**; **See How Much I Love You** by Luis Leante (which limns the deep connection between Spain and its colonies in the Western Sahara); **The Serpent's Daughter**, one of Suzanne Arruda's mysteries (set in 1920) and featuring her regular sleuth Jade del Cameron—this one about a trip to exotic Morocco to reconnect with her mother; Tahir Shah's **In Arabian Nights: A Caravan of Moroccan Dreams**; **The Spy Wore Silk** by Aline, Countess of Romanones; **Stolen Lives: Twenty Years in a Desert Jail** by Malika Oufkir; and Esther Freud's **Hideous Kinky**.

NORWAY: THE LAND OF THE MIDNIGHT SUN

If you've already read Sigrid Undset's great trilogy, **Kristin Lavransdatter** (composed of **The Wreath**, **The Wife**, and **The Cross**) and want to read more of this Nobel Prize–winning writer, you still have ahead of you her other masterpiece, **The Master of Hestviken**. The four books that make up this series include, in order, **The Axe**, **The Snake Pit**, **In the Wilderness**, and **The Son Avenger**. And Undset has still others you might also want to try, including **Return to the Future**, a diary of her escape from Norway after it was invaded by the German army during World War II.

After immersing yourself in medieval Norway, you may want to move right to the more-or-less present, and try these.

The other Norwegian classic writer (and Nobel winner) is Knut Hamsun. I'd begin with **Hunger**, but all his books make for good reading.

Karin Fossum writes dark psychological thrillers; if you're a fan of her fellow Scandinavian Henning Mankell, Fossum is someone to check out. Her novels feature policeman Konrad Sejer, who's introduced to American readers in **Don't Look Back**.

If real noir is to your taste, don't miss the thrillers written by the prize-winning and multitalented Jo (pronounced "Yo") Nesbø; he is also a singer and songwriter for the Norwegian rock group Di Derre. Start with **The Devil's Star**.

In **Out Stealing Horses**, award-winning writer Per Petterson's style is spare and restrained, with a plot that emerges only gradually, and the deliberate pace of the language may force you to read more slowly than usual. From the evocative cover (of the hardback edition) to its exploration of death, grief, forgiveness, and love, this is a novel not to miss. So take a deep breath, settle back in a comfortable chair, and prepare yourself for a beautifully translated, transporting novel about a man reliving his life, especially one particular summer day more than fifty years before. It began when his best friend, Jon, came by with a plan to borrow a neighbor's horses and ended with the realization that nothing would ever be the same, for him or, especially, for Jon, again. If you enjoy this, try Petterson's other novels, including **To Siberia** and **In the Wake**.

Linn Ullman's **Before You Sleep** is the story of the tumultuous Blom family; it's set in both Norway and New York. (The author is

of armchair travel book in which first-world authors spend time in third-world locales, I am always on the lookout for any signs of looking down on, or making fun of, the native populations. Troost is entirely respectful (even when he's describing how corrupt the government is), saving his harshest criticisms for his own fears, inadequacies, and dumb decisions—all of which just made him seem more human to me. Whether it's traversing (or trying to) the mudslick, unpaved roads of the islands; coping with landslides; encountering active volcanoes; discovering giant centipedes seemingly bent on household domination; musing on the pros and cons of cannibalism (while visiting a village in which the last incidence of this practice took place within living memory); surviving Cyclone Paula; or trying out kava, Vanuatu's intoxicating drink of choice, Troost's writing is lively and entertaining. When I finished this book I was sorely tempted to spend my next vacation in Vanuatu and Fiji, but reason belatedly kicked in and I realized that I would probably need to bring Troost himself along as well in order to guarantee myself a good time.

Troost is also the author of **Lost on Planet China: One Man's Attempt to Understand the World's Most Mystifying Nation** and **The Sex Lives of Cannibals: Adrift in the Equatorial Pacific**. What I've discovered in talking to fans of Troost is that their favorite book of his tends to be the first one they read, a fact that's certainly true for me—my first was **Getting Stoned with Savages**, and it remains my favorite.

Arthur Grimble was a British diplomat who was made Resident Commissioner of the Gilbert and Ellice Islands colony in 1926. His two books, **We Chose the Islands: A Six-Year Adventure in** the **Gilberts** and **Return to the Islands**, are about his family's experiences on a set of islands that straddle the equator. Let me just note, I felt more than a little sorry for his wife, despite the fact that Mr. Grimble seemed like a nice enough chap—you had to have a certain quality to be the wife of someone in the British diplomatic service during the heyday of the Empire. Incidentally, you won't find the Gilbert Islands on a recent map—they're now known as the Republic of Kiribati.

The components of Nicholas Drayson's **Confessing a Murder** include a former (fictional) classmate of Charles Darwin, a mysterious scarab, and a marooned man: together they're perfect ingredients for a novel to enjoy, and Drayson does it up beautifully.

And these as well:

> Alexander Frater's **Tales from the Torrid Zone: Travels in the Deep Tropics**
>
> James Michener's **Tales of the South Pacific**, set on the New Hebrides during World War II, is my favorite of all the books he ever wrote; one of the stories in it was the inspiration for *Until They Sail*, one of my best-loved movies.
>
> Charles Montgomery's **The Shark God: Encounters with Ghosts and Ancestors in the South Pacific**
>
> Ronald Wright's **Henderson's Spear** is one of those novels that never got the acclaim it deserved when it was originally published, so read it now!

OHIOANA

Since I spent so much time in 2008 working as a consultant for the Cuyahoga County Public Library, I now consider myself an honorary Ohioan. This, I hasten to tell you, is despite the fact that I graduated from the University of Michigan, a sworn enemy to Ohio State. Oh, those yearly football games! I would actually watch them without a book in hand.

As I think about the books I've read that are set in Ohio, or are written by Ohio authors, these come to mind:

Ruth McKenney's **Industrial Valley** is based around the first wide-scale sit-down strike in labor history—at three tire plants in Akron in the early 1930s. McKenney's depictions of class conflicts at a time when the country was just coming out of the Great Depression are heartfelt and moving. She clearly had an agenda while writing this novel, but I felt that her novel transcended its message. It's a bit ironic that McKenney is probably best known not for this novel, or for **Jake Home** (the story of a labor organizer), but rather for **My Sister Eileen**, a collection of autobiographical stories, originally published in *The New Yorker*, about the adventures of two sisters who move from Ohio to Greenwich Village.

All the Way Home: Building a Family in a Falling-Down House by David Giffels is the story of how a columnist for the *Akron Beacon Journal* (and former writer for *Beavis and Butt-Head*) and his wife restored an old, more-than-a-little-decrepit house that was once owned by a rubber baron. This is more than a do-it-yourself memoir; rather, it's a paean to his hometown.

Crooked River Burning takes place against the backdrop of Cleveland's descent from a major industrial city in the 1940s to a symbol of urban failure by the last decades of the twentieth century. Mark Winegardner interweaves the story of an on-again, off-again years-long relationship between an upper-class girl and her lower-class boyfriend with chapters about major Cleveland movers and shakers, from disc jockey Alan Freed to Carl Stokes, the city's first black mayor.

The Broom of the System was David Foster Wallace's first novel. It's set in a recognizable but clearly not real Cleveland and is marked by Wallace's inventive use of plot, characters, and language. (One of its major characters is a cockatiel named Vlad the Impaler.)

When I was reading Don Robertson's **The Greatest Thing Since Sliced Bread**, I found myself alternating between laughter and tears, and I knew I would never forget the young hero, nine-year-old Morris Bird III (whom some classmates unkindly call Morris Bird the Turd). One autumn day in 1944 he walks across Cleveland to visit his best friend, Stanley Chaloupka. He sets off with an alarm clock, a jar of Peter Pan peanut butter, a map, a compass, a dollar and some change, and (most reluctantly) his six-year-old sister, Sandra. Along the way he gets delayed by a cigarette riot and Sandra's whining insistence that she be allowed to play a game of jacks. He also dropkicks a football into a coal wagon (much to the annoyance of the football's young owners), is rescued by Miss Edna Daphne Frost, and eventually, as the afternoon winds down, Morris and Sandra collide with history. They arrive at Stanley's block at the exact moment when above-ground gas tanks belonging to the East Ohio Gas Company explode. (The explosion and subsequent fire would kill over one hundred people and destroy a full square mile of Cleveland's east side.) I loved this slim novel when it was first published in the early '60s; I am just thrilled that a whole new generation of readers is now going to get to read it, too.

OXFORD

I think I fell in love with Oxford the first time I read Dorothy Sayers's **Gaudy Night** way back when I was in college; I've never fallen out of love with the city (or that novel). Even a "real life" visit didn't dim my ardor. And judging by the number of books that evoke the spirit and sense of the place that Matthew Arnold called "that sweet city with her dreaming spires," I'm not alone. You have a wide choice in reading here—nonfiction, mysteries, and literary fiction about the place abound. Here are some that I've particularly enjoyed.

Nonfiction

Two good places to begin to get an overview of the city are **The Oxford Book of Oxford**, edited by Jan Morris, and David Horan's **Oxford: A Cultural and Literary Companion**. Both are filled with good bits of history and lively anecdotes. Horan's is loosely arranged by the many well-known people whose lives touched the city or the colleges—from Charles I, who holed up in Christ Church (the largest of all Oxford Colleges) when he was trying to escape from Parliament, to the novelist John Buchan (**The Thirty-Nine Steps**) and Nobel Prize–winner William Golding (**Lord of the Flies**), who were both Brasenose lads. Ved Mehta's **Up at Oxford** is one of the author's series of memoirs, and, I think, his best. It's a splendid picture of Oxford in the 1950s, told in Mehta's unique voice. Then there's Justin Cartwright's **Oxford Revisited**, in which the novelist looks back on his student years there.

Mysteries

Guillermo Martínez's **The Oxford Murders** (one of those cerebral puzzles that always make me wish I were smarter than I am); **The September Society** by Charles Finch; Colin Dexter's series featuring the irascible Oxford policeman, Inspector Morse, and his trusty sidekick, Sergeant Lewis—two of my favorites are early ones, **Last Bus to Woodstock** and **The Silent World of Nicholas Quinn**; and Edmund Crispin's series of puzzlers featuring Gervase Fen, an Oxford don who keeps stumbling across murders. **The Case of the Gilded Fly** is one of the best, **The Moving Toyshop** is my favorite, and **The Glimpses of the Moon** is a humorous treat. (And there are a few more in the all-too-short series, as well.)

Literary Fiction

Javier Marías's **All Souls**, which begins with "Oxford is, without a doubt, one of the cities of the world where the least work gets done"; Melanie Benjamin's **Alice I Have Been** (a well-wrought fictional retelling of Alice's relationship with Lewis Carroll); the satirical

Zuleika Dobson by Max Beerbohm; **Brideshead Revisited** by Evelyn Waugh; Philip Larkin's **Jill**; **Where the Rivers Meet** and sequels by John Wain (lots on the town vs. gown division); **Jane and Prudence** by Barbara Pym; and **The Temple** by Stephen Spender.

But I defy anyone to read **Oxford**, James (now Jan) Morris's book, originally published in 1965 and reprinted in 2001, and not want to go there for a long stay, immediately. History, biography, literature: the whole ambiance of the city is engagingly presented.

PARMA

One of my teachers at St. John's College recommended **The Charterhouse of Parma** to me. It took more decades than I care to admit to finally get around to reading it, but I have to say that finally reading Stendhal's novel was a revelation—it's a book of love and passion in the late nineteenth century in Northern Italy that doesn't minimize the complications that come along with those feelings. I read the translation by Richard Howard, but probably every reader will have his or her favorite. (Incidentally, it wasn't until I was writing this section that I realized that I didn't know what Stendhal's first name was and learned, via Wikipedia, that Stendhal was a pseudonym for Marie-Henri Beyle.)

John Grisham eschewed courtroom thrillers and young lawyers choosing the wrong law firm to join in **Playing for Pizza**, a captivating novel about Rick Dockery, a pro quarterback who—as a result of having a very bad day on the football field during the AFC championship—goes to play for the Parma Panthers and learns there's more to Italy than pizza, despite the title. In fact, one of the things Rick learns is that it's important to pace yourself through those multiple-course Italian meals.

PATAGONIA

Patagonia might someday be its own country but for now it's partly in Argentina and partly in Chile, in the southern-most parts of both countries. I must warn you that once you start reading about Patagonia it's hard to stop, because it's been the scene of such diverse events: for years Butch Cassidy and the Sundance Kid hid out from the Pinkertons there; rumors abounded that creatures who were well known in prehistoric times were now being glimpsed roaming the wilderness; Welsh and Jewish settlements were common; and gauchos rode to glory on the pampas. Here are the best books I've found.

Probably the granddaddy of writers who described their days in Patagonia is W. H. Hudson. (He may be best known for **Green Mansions: A Romance of the Tropical Forest**—remember Rima the Bird-girl?—but that takes place in Guyana, not Patagonia.) His Patagonian book—heavy on the bird life there—is **Idle Days in Patagonia**.

In Patagonia by Bruce Chatwin is probably the one book every Patagonian traveler takes along with him or her; second choice, not far behind, is Paul Theroux's **The Old Patagonian Express**. (Incidentally, if Chatwin's life interests you, don't neglect **Bruce Chatwin: A Biography** by Nicholas Shakespeare.)

Speaking (even parenthetically) of Nicholas Shakespeare, in his introduction to the Penguin Classics edition of Chatwin's **In Patagonia**, he has this to say: "In Patagonia, the isolation makes it easy to exaggerate the person you are: the drinker drinks; the devout prays; the lonely grows lonelier; sometimes fatally." I don't know, but it doesn't seem a far leap to imagine that Robert Kull had the same sort of notion in mind when he wrote his doctoral dissertation on the effects of deep wilderness solitude on a human being. His research resulted in **Solitude: Seeking Wisdom in Extremes: A Year Alone in the Patagonia Wilderness**, a book that is a lesson to anyone who thinks that being alone with one's thoughts for an extended period is in any way easy.

Nick Reding's **The Last Cowboys at the End of the World: The Story of the Gauchos of Patagonia** convinced me that the world is not quite as tamed as most people think it to be—there are still unusual lives to be lived, and unusual places to live them.

There's also a gripping section in Michael Novacek's **Time Traveler: In Search of Dinosaurs and Ancient Mammals from Montana to Mongolia** about hunting for whale fossils in Patagonia.

For fiction (and there's not a lot available), try Richard Llewellyn's sequels to **How Green Was My Valley**: **Up, into the Singing Mountain**, and **Down Where the Moon Is Small** (sometimes called **And I Shall Sleep . . . Down Where the Moon Is Small**), both about his hero Huw's life in Argentinian Patagonia.

PEACE CORPS MEMORIES

In the fall of 1960, at a speech at the University of Michigan, President John F. Kennedy outlined his ideas for what would shortly become the Peace Corps. Little did anyone realize at the time that one unexpected outcome of the project would be a lot of good reading, in the form of memoirs by former Peace Corps volunteers. Here are some I'd recommend.

Jeanne D'Haem's **The Last Camel: True Stories of Somalia**

Sarah Erdman's **Nine Hills to Nambonkaha: Two Years in the Heart of an African Village** (Ivory Coast)

Susana Herrera's **Mango Elephants in the Sun: How Life in an African Village Let Me Be in My Skin** (Northern Cameroon)

Peter Hessler's **River Town: Two Years on the Yangtze** (China, of course)

Kris Holloway's **Monique and the Mango Rains: Two Years with a Midwife in Mali** (more fully described in the "Timbuktu and Beyond" section)

Hilary Liftin and Kate Montgomery's **Dear Exile: The True Story of Two Friends Separated (for a**

Year) by an Ocean (letters between two college friends, written when one was in Kenya [Kate] and one was trying to make a life in Manhattan [Hilary])

George Packer's **The Village of Waiting** (Togo, West Africa)

Josh Swiller's **The Unheard: A Memoir of Deafness and Africa** tells of his experiences as a deaf Peace Corps volunteer in an out-of-the-way village in Zambia.

Moritz Thomsen's **Living Poor: A Peace Corps Chronicle** was one of the first published accounts by a Peace Corps volunteer; it remains one of the best. And, if you're going to just read one book on the topic, make it this one. It's realistic, painful, and somehow ennobling in its descriptions of Peace Corps life in Ecuador. There's another superb book of Thomsen's described in the "Brazil" section.

Mike Tidwell's **The Ponds of Kalambayi** (Zaire)

Tom Bissell hasn't written what could be called a memoir of his experiences as a PCV in Central Asia, but it's certainly informed several of his other books, including **Chasing the Sea: Lost Among the Ghosts of Empire in Central Asia** and **God Lives in St. Petersburg and Other Stories**.

PERU(SING) PERU

When you think of Peru, probably the first thing that comes to mind is Machu Picchu, one of the last strongholds of the Incan Empire in the sixteenth century. Present-day travelers to Peru may want to read about the history of Peru but should also take a look at contemporary works. Here are some suggestions for both.

Of the three major histories of the Spanish conquest of Peru (William Prescott's **History of the Conquest of Peru**, originally published in 1847; John Hemming's **The Conquest of the Incas**, which came out in 1970; and Kim MacQuarrie's **The Last Days of the Incas**, published in 2007), Prescott's is magisterial and weighty, Hemming's is considered by many the definitive contemporary account, and MacQuarrie's is eminently readable.

Yet another classic is Yale explorer Hiram Bingham's **Lost City of the Incas**. (He's often considered to be the basis for the fictional explorer/adventurer Indiana Jones.) Although there's an ongoing kerfuffle over Bingham's exact role in "discovering" Macchu Picchu, and there's a lawsuit in place to force Yale to return the artifacts that Bingham brought home, we shouldn't let that stop us from reading his accounts of the country whose history he loved.

The newest biography of Bingham is **Cradle of Gold: The Story of Hiram Bingham, a Real-Life Indiana Jones, and the Search for Machu Picchu** by Christopher Heaney.

Hugh Thomson is a great storyteller, and his book **The White Rock** is a perfect mixture of history, geography, and sightseeing in the Peruvian Andes, framed around a search for the lost Inca city of

Llactapata. And you can't do better than his **A Sacred Landscape: The Search for Ancient Peru**, which considers what's changed and what's remained mostly the same in the five or so centuries since the end of the Incan empire.

Take a look at these, too: Tobias Schneebaum's **Keep the River on Your Right** and Dervla Murphy's **Eight Feet in the Andes: Travels with a Mule in Unknown Peru**, in which the unfaltering traveler leaves her home in Ireland for a trip to South America, accompanied by her daughter and the animal mentioned in the title.

Novels by non-Peruvians that illuminate Peruvian history and culture include Thornton Wilder's classic **The Bridge of San Luis Rey**; Ruthanne Lum McCunn's **God of Luck** (about a little-known historical event—the kidnapping, between 1840 and 1875, of close to a million Chinese men who were then sold into slavery in South America); **The Vision of Elena Silves** by Nicholas Shakespeare; **To the Last City** by Colin Thubron, which was shortlisted for the Man Booker Prize in 2002 and takes place in the ruins of an Inca city in Peru; and Henry Shukman's **The Lost City**.

Good reads by Peruvian writers include: Daniel Alarcón's fiction—both his novel **Lost City Radio** and **War By Candlelight**, a collection of stories—and José María Arguedas's autobiographical **Deep Rivers** (with a terrific translation by Frances Horning Barraclough that won the 1978 Translation Center Award from Columbia University).

PHILADELPHIA

When I started to think about which of my favorite novels take place in the City of Brotherly Love, I discovered that they generally fell into two groups: mysteries/thrillers and sports.

Here are the mysteries/thrillers:

I have recently become addicted to Jane Haddam's books, which are all set in an Armenian American section of Philadelphia and feature retired FBI agent Gregor Demarkian. Once I read 2009's **Living Witness**, I went back and avidly read twenty-two or so that I had unaccountably missed. Haddam's books aren't for thriller readers looking for adrenaline-charged page-turners; they're truly character-driven, deliciously slow-paced, and intricately plotted. Although events in Gregor's personal life change and develop over the course of the two dozen books, I don't think it's necessary to read them in order. (The earliest ones are a bear to find.) Two other recent entries in the series that I'd highly recommend are **The Headmaster's Wife** and **Cheating at Solitaire**.

Victor Carl is the main character in a series of novels by William Lashner. How could anyone resist a dubious hero who frequently resorts to "yowza" and "gad" to express his feelings? Not me. Carl's not a particularly successful attorney, always teetering on the edge of going broke, so he's frequently forced to take cases no one else will, and he's not above using deceit, dodgy ethics, and downright trickery to get his clients off. One of my favorites is **A Killer's Kiss**. As in all of the Victor Carl mysteries, the plot is satisfyingly complex, making it almost impossible for anyone (except Victor) to finally figure out whodunit.

Gillian Roberts has written many mysteries about schoolteacher Amanda Pepper. The first one is **Caught Dead in Philadelphia**, and they're all perfect for cozy mystery fans.

Bennie Rosato, the Philadelphia attorney who stars in Lisa Scottoline's series has a particularly tough time of it in **Mistaken Identity**, because there's a woman out there who swears she's Bennie's long-lost twin sister.

And here are two books—one fiction and one nonfiction—that showcase Philadelphia's love for its football team, the Eagles:

Matthew Quick's **The Silver Linings Playbook** is a heart-warming, humorous, and soul-satisfying first novel (but not at all soppy or overly sweet, I promise). The main character is thirty-year-old Pat Peoples, a former high school history teacher, who believes in happy endings and silver linings—despite the fact that his father won't even talk to him, there are huge gaps in his memory, and he's become addicted to working out. As Pat slowly begins to remember and come to terms with the painful realities of his past, he's aided by an eccentric (but effective) psychiatrist named Patel (who shares Pat's love for the Eagles) and Tiffany, the widowed sister-in-law of his old best friend, Ronnie.

It's probably enough to say that the content of Jere Longman's **If Football's a Religion, Why Don't We Have a Prayer?: Philadelphia, Its Faithful, and the Eternal Quest for Sports Salvation** is as entertaining as the title.

But there are a few novels about Philadelphia that have nothing to do with either sports or crime:

Lorene Cary's moving historical novel, **The Price of a Child**

Richard Powell's **The Philadelphian** (which was made into one of my very favorite movies; it was called *The Young Philadelphians* and starred a very young Paul Newman and Gig Young)

John Edgar Wideman's **Philadelphia Fire** (and all his others)

And last, probably the most unusual novel about Philadelphia I expect we'll ever encounter is Kathryn Davis's **Hell**. You never know quite what to expect from Davis, but in this, her third exceptionally well-written work, she really outdoes herself.

POLISH UP YOUR POLISH

Books about Poland—both fiction and nonfiction—don't often have the happiest of themes. It's a country that's been buffeted by history. Or maybe swamped is a better choice of verb. There are memoirs beyond number, oodles of histories (frequently offering contradictory interpretations of the past, especially as it relates to World War II and the treatment of Polish Jews), and fiction from eminent writers such as the Singer brothers (Isaac Bashevis and Israel Joshua), Jerzy Kosiński, the science fiction writer Stanislaw Lem, as well as poetry from the likes of Czeslaw Milosz and Wislawa Szymborska. It's quite clear that if you want to read Polish writers and/or books set in Poland before you actually go there, you'd better start early and plan on reading late into many a night.

Here are some titles that I've been either entertained or moved by: Brigid Pasulka's **A Long Long Time Ago and Essentially True** is set in both the Krakow of the early 1990s, shortly after the fall of the Berlin Wall, and the Poland of World War II. It's a story of war, love, and the way the human spirit can triumph over unlikely odds. It was a pleasure to read. Fans of **The Guernsey Literary and Potato Peel Pie Society** by Mary Ann Shaffer and Annie Barrows and **Major Pettigrew's Last Stand** by Helen Simonson won't want to miss it.

For a sweeping overview of Poland's history—especially good if you aren't demanding fine writing and three-dimensional characters—try James Michener's **Poland**.

Czeslaw Milosz turned to prose in **Legends of Modernity: Essays and Letters from Occupied Poland, 1942–43**, which offers readers an up-close and personal account of life in Warsaw under Nazi rule.

The beautiful writing of **The Zoo-Keeper's Wife** by Diane Ackerman illuminates the true story of Warsaw zookeepers Jan and Antonina Zabinski, who together contrived to save hundreds of lives during World War II. This is a must-read.

Other books about Poland, both its past and its present, include: Nonfiction: Michael Moran's **A Country in the Moon: Travels in Search of the Heart of Poland**; **The Lost: A Search for Six of Six Million** by Daniel Mendelsohn is revelatory; Eva Hoffman's **Shtetl: The Life and Death of a Small Town and the World of Polish Jews** (I read—with great admiration—

everything that Hoffman writes); Adam Zagajewski's **Another Beauty**; and Nobel Prize–winning Isaac Bashevis Singer's memoir **In My Father's Court**.

Fiction: **Madame: A Novel** by Antoni Libera (Soviet-era Poland); Louis Begley's **Wartime Lies**; Charles T. Powers's **In the Memory of the Forest**; Jane Yolen's **Briar Rose** (ostensibly a book for teens, but it's perfect for any age); Anne Michaels's **Fugitive Pieces** (at least the first half); Lilian Nattel's **The River Midnight**; **Trans-Atlantyk** by Witold Gombrowicz (or any other of his autobiographical novels); and Alan Furst's **The Spies of Warsaw**. Furst's novels are great for their splendid sense of place—World War II Eastern Europe.

POSTCARDS FROM MEXICO

The title of this section is the name of one of my favorite songs by the group Girlyman. (At one point I wanted to use song titles for all the sections, but gave it up as an impossible dream.)

Any stray thoughts I might have entertained of going anyplace in Mexico besides Oaxaca, Cuernevaca, and Mazatlan immediately vanished upon reading **God's Middle Finger: Into the Lawless Heart of the Sierra Madre** by Richard Grant. Not that I regret reading it—to the contrary, it's a mesmerizing account of one of the most dangerous areas in North America, where drug growers, buyers, and sellers are prevalent, murders are many, and the folklore of the place is difficult to separate from the facts (think Humphrey Bogart, the Apaches, and Pancho Villa). But I have to say that sharing Grant's (often harebrained) adventures through the pages of this book is adventure enough for me.

Charles Bowden's **Murder City: Ciudad Juárez and the Global Economy's New Killing Fields** also shook me to the core. It describes how this city—right across the Rio Grande from El Paso—continues to disintegrate into an anarchy of crime and violence.

But on to happier books:

The Copper Canyons in the Sierra Madre provide much of the setting for **Born to Run: A Hidden Tribe, Super Athletes, and the Greatest Race the World Has Never Seen** by Christopher McDougall. It's a must-read for runners, of course, but even non-runners should find it interesting, as it includes other topics as well, especially an introduction to the little known and understood Tarahumara Indians, their beliefs, culture, and way of life. I especially enjoyed McDougall's chatty and yet informative writing style.

Bruce Chatwin (no slouch as a travel writer himself, of course) called Sybille Bedford's **A Visit to Don Otavio: A Traveller's Tale from Mexico** one of the best travel books of the twentieth century. Set right after World War II, it's a sublimely well-written portrait of the country.

Nonfiction fans will also want to take a look at these: Octavio Paz's **The Labyrinth of Solitude** is a 1950s book that helps us get a handle on the country even today—half a century later; Alan Riding's **Distant Neighbors: A Portrait of the Mexicans** is also many years old now—it was published in 1989—but it still makes excellent reading for anyone interested in trying to understand how Mexico's past is informing its present; Earl Shorris's **The Life and Times of Mexico** is a well-written narrative history; Tony Cohan's eminently readable **Mexican Days: Journeys into the Heart of Mexico**; and Rebecca West's **Survivors in Mexico**, which explores—with her usual panache—the dark clash between the Aztecs and the Spaniards. Finally, Graham Greene's **The Lawless Roads** explores Mexican attitudes in the tumultuous 1930s—the research and travel that went into writing this book provided Greene with the setting for one of his best novels, **The Power and the Glory**.

Who knew that the renowned neurologist Oliver Sacks (author of, among many other books, **The Man Who Mistook His Wife for A Hat and Other Clinical Tales**) was also a fern fanatic? I certainly didn't, until I picked up his **Oaxaca Journal**, a charming account of fern hunting in Southern Mexico. Another book set in Oaxaca is Peter Kuper's **Diario de Oaxaca: A Sketchbook Journal of Two Years in Mexico**. As a friend wrote me, "it gives an earthy and organic feel to what living in Oaxaca can be like. It combines a journalistic eye for political events with the close-up gaze of a people (and bug) watcher." All true.

Following hard on the heels of two well-reviewed titles (the novel **The Hummingbird's Daughter** and the nonfiction work **The Devil's Highway**), Luis Alberto Urrea once again scores high with **Into the Beautiful North**, in which nineteen-year-old Nayeli, who works at a taco stand in a small coastal Mexican village called Tres Camarones, decides to travel to the United States to find her father and bring him home. The characters are three-dimensional (especially Nayeli); the plot is fast paced and filled, somewhat unexpectedly, given the subject, with humor. Book clubs, especially those interested in reading multicultural novels, will want to add this to their list of books to be discussed.

And these:

Sandra Benítez's **A Place Where the Sea Remembers**; **Consider This, Señora**, an unforgettable novel by Harriet Doerr; the first half, especially, of Barbara Kingsolver's **The Lacuna**, which includes wonderfully nuanced portraits of Diego Rivera, Frieda Kahlo, and Leon Trotsky; **Amigoland**, Oscar Casares's warm and funny story of two aged brothers who take a road trip to Mexico to try to find out—at long last—the true story of their grandfather's kidnapping; **News from the Empire** by one of Mexico's best writers, Fernando Del Paso; and last, but not at all least, Malcolm Lowry's **Under the Volcano**, which has always struck me as being the über viscerally painful novel.

PROVENCE AND THE SOUTH OF FRANCE

For anyone going to spend time in the south of France, Peter Mayle's **A Year in Provence** is a good place to start. But don't stop there: all of the following books—as different as they may seem—make superb armchair reading. And they're good to take with you, should you actually be traveling.

Ford Madox Ford's **Provence** is a lovingly written account of *la vie bohème*, as lived by Ford and his artist lover, Biala, in Provence during the 1920s. It seems to be written by a different man than the one who began **The Good Soldier**, his novel of passion and betrayal, with the sentence "This is the saddest story I have ever heard." Incidentally, when Ford's **Provence** was published both Graham Greene and Dorothy Parker found it to be splendid—and that's a most unlikely pairing of critics!

Two Towns in Provence by M. F. K. Fisher contains two of her most appealing memoirs: **Map of Another Town** (about Aix-en-Provence) and **A Considerable Town** (an appreciation of Marseille).

The selections in **Travelers' Tales: Provence**, edited by James O'Reilly and Tara Austen Weaver, remind me of the amuse-bouche that a chef will sometimes send out to diners: small tastes that indicate the quality of the rest of the meal.

Fiction fans should check out these:

Jean Giono, born in Provence in 1895, gives readers a joyous sense of the Provençal countryside in many of his novels, including my favorite, **Joy of Man's Desiring**, although he's probably best known for his short story, "The Man Who Planted Trees."

I am a huge fan of award-winning Canadian writer Guy Gavriel Kay. I love the way he writes very realistic novels with just a bit of fantasy thrown in. I'd urge you to read **The Lions of Al-Rassan**, **The Last Light of the Sun**, or **Under Heaven**. But since we're talking of Provence here, don't miss **Ysabel**. Although it's mostly set in twenty-first-century Aix-en-Provence, there's enough history and adventure to satisfy even non-fantasy fans.

Madam, Will You Talk was Mary Stewart's first work of romantic suspense, and if that's your fiction genre of choice, it's a classic.

Not only is there the requisite romance and suspense, but Stewart gives us a palpable sense of the city of Marseille.

I was quite taken with the tale of American poet W. S. Merwin's purchase of a ruined house in the rural province of Quercy, which he recounts in the more-or-less autobiographical grouping of three stories in **The Lost Upland: Stories of Southwestern France**.

History fans will want to take a look at these two books:

Four Queens: The Provençal Sisters Who Ruled Europe by Nancy Goldstone is a captivating overview of the daughters of the King and Queen of Provence—Marguerite, Eleanor, Beatrice, and Sanchia—and their memorable marriages, which, together, shaped thirteenth-century Europe.

Lawrence Durrell's **Caesar's Vast Ghost: Aspects of Provence** is an assortment of history, literature, cultural commentary, and diary-like entries.

ROMAN HOLIDAY

To really understand contemporary Rome, I think it's necessary to get a feel for its storied past. There are, of course, more histories written of Rome and its Empire than anyone could probably get to in one lifetime, but I'd actually give those a miss (unless you're *really* interested, and in that case I'd read anything that Michael Grant wrote about the city), and head instead for Colleen McCullough's Masters of Rome series. They are, in order, **The First Man in Rome, The Grass Crown, Fortune's Favorites, Caesar's Women, Caesar, The October Horse**, and **Antony and Cleopatra**.

There are several terrific series of mystery novels set in Ancient Rome—check out the novels of Steven Saylor and Lindsey Davis. I've always felt, in fact, that after reading all of the Saylor and Davis books I could easily get an advanced degree in Roman history.

Anthony Doerr's **Four Seasons in Rome: On Twins, Insomnia, and the Biggest Funeral in the History of the World** is pure delight, and not only for new parents, those with a trip to Rome in their immediate future, or somebody trying to write a novel.

Paul Hofmann, onetime bureau chief for the *New York Times*, spent more than thirty years living in the Eternal City. His descriptions of people and places, and—what I found immensely interesting—the art of living in Rome make **The Seasons of Rome: A Journal** worth seeking out.

Other books for the traveler to Rome include **Rome from the Ground Up** by James H. S. McGregor (great for architecture and history buffs); **Rome and a Villa** by Eleanor Clark; Jonathan Boardman's **Rome: A Cultural and Literary Companion**; Margaret Visser's study of the Sant'Agnese fuori le Mura church, **The Geometry of Love: Space, Time, Mystery, and Meaning in an Ordinary Church**; and **A Traveller in Rome** by H. V. Morton.

Gritty-mystery aficionados should check out **The Dogs of Rome: A Commissario Alec Blume Novel**, the first in a projected series by Conor Fitzgerald. We're introduced to Blume as he works on a particularly inept murder that leads into an increasingly complex investigation.

ROW, ROW, ROW YOUR BOAT

According to the *New York Times*, 1896 was a good year for rowers. It was the first time that anyone managed to cross the Atlantic in an open boat: George Harbo and Gabriel Samuelson rowed from New York to France. The next time that feat was accomplished was seven decades later.

Tori Murden McClure is an incredibly accomplished woman with many degrees and good jobs, and she definitely fits in this category because she was the first woman to row—solo—across the Atlantic Ocean. The story of how—and why—she chose to attempt the crossing (twice, actually, since her first trip was halted by a hurricane) is uplifting without being at all sappy. I loved the first line: "In the end, I know I rowed across the Atlantic to find my heart, but in the beginning, I wasn't aware that it was missing." And I was taken by the fact that it was Muhammad Ali who encouraged her to try the solo crossing a second time, by saying to her that she didn't want to be the first woman who "almost rowed across the Atlantic." She describes her journey(s) in **A Pearl in the Storm: How I Found My Heart in the Middle of the Ocean**.

Other courageous rowers have written about their trips in these enjoyable and sometimes heart-stopping accounts:

Both **Challenging the Pacific: The First Woman to Row the Kon-Tiki Route** and **Across the Savage Sea: The First Woman to Row Across the North Atlantic** by Maud Fontenoy are well worth your reading time.

Jill Fredston's accounts of her and her husband's self-propelled journeys to some of the most remote places they could find are well told in **Rowing to Latitude: Journeys Along the Arctic's Edge**. (When they're not rowing, Jill and her husband, Doug Fesler, research avalanches and train rescuers. Their experiences doing that would make another great book.)

Between them, Colin and Julie Angus have written several books about their rowing experiences, both together and apart, including these two: **Rowed Trip: From Scotland to Syria by Oar**, which describes their trips to countries far and near, including an effort to rediscover their ancestral homes; and an account of Julie's unaccompanied adventure, **Rowboat in a Hurricane: My Amazing Journey Across a Changing Atlantic Ocean**.

In Roz Savage's **Rowing the Atlantic: Lessons Learned on the Open Ocean**, she writes about her experience as the only solo female contestant in the 2005 Atlantic Rowing Race, which she entered despite having little previous rowing experience. Here's one of the best lines—or a least one that shows she maintained her sense of humor despite the pain and the dangers that beset her: "I loved the solitude, the wildness, the beauty. But the ocean and I would have got along better if she would stop trying to get in the boat with me."

Bus, Boat, and Camel. The latter is a thoughtful description of his (sometimes torturous) travel through the Sahel—the countries that border the Sahara desert, including Chad, Nigeria, Niger, and Mali. His prose is fluent, his descriptions are powerful, and his accounts of the people he meets—both Muslim and not—are especially meaningful in our post-9/11 world.

SAINT PETERSBURG/
LENINGRAD/SAINT PETERSBURG

Leningrad, which returned to its traditional, pre-communist name of Saint Petersburg in 1991, underwent a terrible siege during World War II. It was an ultimately unsuccessful attempt by the Germans and the Axis powers to bring Russia and its allies to their collective knees by starving out the residents of Leningrad in the fall and winter of 1941–42. Unsuccessful it might have been, but it was hell on earth for the people living in the starving city. Here are four books—three novels and the authoritative history—on the event, plus a new translation of a classic.

In Debra Dean's first novel **The Madonnas of Leningrad**, Marina works as a tour guide at the Hermitage Museum, where the staff, fearing the onslaught of German troops, begins to dismantle the museum by taking down the paintings but leaving their frames hanging. To hold onto her sanity while her life is almost quite literally deconstructing around her, Marina memorizes the holdings of the museum, room by remarkable room, to create her own personal "memory palace." It's to these memories that Marina returns as her grip on the present becomes ever more tenuous. After finishing the book I felt as though I'd had a long visit to the Hermitage, wandering through its unrivalled collection.

Leningrad during the siege may seem to be a strange setting for a novel that is best described as a lively, good-hearted buddy tale, but there it is, and if you enjoy the élan of movies like *Butch Cassidy and the Sundance Kid* and *The Sting*, here's the novelistic equivalent. (When I told a friend how much I enjoyed reading David Benioff's **City of Thieves**, he replied that he bet there was already a screenplay of it in the hands of the young actor Shia LaBoeuf. I can but hope that it's true, because it would make a most enjoyable film.) The novel begins with a visit between the author and his grandfather. David Benioff presses his elderly relative for information about what happened to him during the siege; what follows the first chapter is his grandfather's tale. But there's a catch. How reliable is the older man's story? When David tries to get answers to some of his specific questions, his grandfather tells him that since he's a writer, he should just make it up. So how much is truth and how much fiction? Maybe ultimately it doesn't matter.

The Siege, Helen Dunmore's sharply observed and painful story of a love affair set against the devastation wrought by the German advance on the city, is one of those unforgettable novels that knocks your socks off with its gorgeous writing.

Harrison Salisbury's comprehensive but very readable nonfiction account, **The 900 Days: The Siege of Leningrad**, will tell you all you ever wanted to know—and perhaps more—about its subject. Despite its age (it was published in 1985) it remains a valuable read.

As for getting a sense of the city before World War II, try the glorious new translation of **Anna Karenina** by Richard Pevear and

Larissa Volokhonsky, which is set in both nineteenth-century Saint Petersburg and Moscow.

SAN FRANCISCO

I am so happy that Chicago Review Press has begun reissuing Gwen Bristow's historical romances. They're just as good as I remember them being, back when I first read them eons ago. **Calico Palace** takes place in San Francisco in 1848, just before gold was discovered at Sutter's Mill on the south fork of the American River. The portrait of the city in its infancy is three-dimensional; the lives of the characters animate the various social classes and occupations in this city of only nine hundred (white) residents.

One of the major events in San Francisco history is, of course, the great earthquake of 1906, and one of the best—if not *the* best—books about it is Simon Winchester's **A Crack in the Edge of the World: America and the Great California Earthquake of 1906**.

John Miller edited **San Francisco Stories: Great Writers on the City**, an anthology that includes essays, poetry, and excerpts from longer works. Contributors include a wide range of names, from Jack Kerouac to Amy Tan to Randy Shilts, and very many different aspects of the city are covered. It's a grand introduction.

Randy Shilts wrote **The Mayor of Castro Street: The Life and Times of Harvey Milk**, which incorporates local history and politics, the biography of Milk, and an overview of the gay community in the 1940s and '50s. (If you enjoyed the movie *Milk*, you'll like the book a lot.) This was Shilts's first book; it's probably not quite as well known as his **And the Band Played On: Politics,**

People, and the AIDS Epidemic. Shilts was a wonderful writer, and died much too young.

One of Laurie R. King's two mystery series takes place in San Francisco. Kate Martinelli is a San Francisco detective, and her cases range from investigating the death of a Sherlock Holmes fan to that of a homeless man. The first is **A Grave Talent**.

Gus Lee's **China Boy** is a great coming-of-age novel set in 1950s San Francisco.

And don't miss out on Armistead Maupin's Tales of the City series. These you will want to read in order, so begin with **Tales of the City** and then go on to **More Tales of the City**.

SCENES FROM SRI LANKA

Michael Ondaatje called Sri Lanka "that pendant off the ear of India," and here are some excellent books about the country for your reading pleasure.

Adele Barker's **Not Quite Paradise: An American Sojourn in Sri Lanka** describes the author's Fulbright year teaching at the University of Peradeniya.

Tea Time with Terrorists: A Motorcycle Journey into the Heart of Sri Lanka's Civil War by Mark Stephen Meadows gives you a good sense of a beautiful country that has been wracked by thirty years of a complex civil war.

In **When Memory Dies** by A. Sivanandan, three generations of a Sri Lankan family try to make sense of not only their personal relationships, but also what is happening to their country as it devolves into a tripartite, seemingly endless war.

excellent books about her, the first nonfiction and the second fiction: Antonia Fraser's **Mary Queen of Scots** (any of Fraser's biographies are worth reading) and Margaret George's **Mary Queen of Scotland and the Isles** (any of the fictional biographies and autobiographies by George are also worth reading).

To get a sense of the wide range of Scottish fiction over the years, try these: **Rob Roy** (and others) by Sir Walter Scott (of course); Denise Mina's Glasgow-based crime novels, such as **Slip of the Knife** (be forewarned: they're dark); Val McDermid's **A Darker Domain**, in which Cold Case Review Team Inspector Karen Pirie deals with two seemingly unrelated cases from the 1980s; Andrew O'Hagan's **Our Fathers**; **A Scots Quair**, a trilogy by Lewis Grassic Gibbon that includes **Sunset Song**, **Cloud Howe**, and **Grey Granite**; **The Citadel** by A. J. Cronin; Louise Welsh's **The Cutting Room**; Irvine Welsh's **Trainspotting** (not an easy book to read, because it takes a while to get used to the way Welsh adapts language, but many people believe it's the most important Scottish novel of the twentieth century); Alexander McCall Smith's two entertaining series set in Scotland, the Isabel Dalhousie mysteries (the first is **The Sunday Philosophy Club**) and the Scotland Street novels (the first is **44 Scotland Street**); Sara Maitland's **Ancestral Truths**, which mostly takes place in Scotland, although an important part is set in Zimbabwe; and Ali Smith's **The Accidental** and **Hotel World**.

I haven't listed any of the many romance novels that take place in Scotland because there's a whole book waiting to be written (but not by me) about stories of those hunky men, their kilts, and the women who love them. Let one name suffice for all: Diana

Gabaldon. But if there's a particular romance writer you adore, the chances are good that one or more of his or her books take place in Scotland. Ask your local librarian for help in finding them.

SEE THE SEA

I hope that I read this in a book and it didn't really happen to me, but I fear it did. I should say at once that I have never understood what to do in a sailboat when the wind picks up, despite having it explained to me numerous times. When I was in college, one of my earliest experiences sailing was on the Severn River, and in very short order everything went wrong: big wind, boat capsizing, mast breaking. That's the part I remember (or think I remember), but I have no memory of what came next, although I clearly lived to tell the tale. Not everyone is so lucky. Here are some books about sailors whose grasp of the fundamentals is much better than mine . . . and many of whose outcomes were far worse.

> **Always a Distant Anchorage** by Hal Roth is the perfect choice for those who dream of one big voyage under sail.
>
> **At the Mercy of the Sea: The True Story of Three Sailors in a Caribbean Hurricane** and **Flirting with Mermaids**, both by John Kretschmer

Berserk: My Voyage to the Antarctic in a Twenty-Seven-Foot Sailboat by David Mercy (not a pleasure trip)

Endurance: Shackleton's Incredible Voyage by Alfred Lansing

Fair Wind and Plenty of It: A Modern-Day Tall Ship Adventure by Rigel Crockett is the tale of the crew and passengers of the *Picton Castle*, a three-masted tall ship, and its eighteen-month voyage around the world. It's the story of two obsessions: that of the Nova Scotia–born author who grew up in a sailboat-fixated family, and of Captain Dan Moreland, who turned an almost seventy-year-old North Sea trawler into a tall ship in order to emulate the great sailing captains of the past.

Fastnet, Force 10: The Deadliest Storm in the History of Modern Sailing by John Rousmaniere

In **The Greatest Sailing Stories Ever Told: Twenty-Seven Unforgettable Stories**, edited by Christopher Caswell, you'll find familiar and unfamiliar names and tales.

Maiden Voyage by Tania Aebi

Pacific Lady: The First Woman to Sail Solo Across the World's Largest Ocean by Sharon Sites Adams with Karen Coates

Sailing Alone Around the World by Joshua Slocum along with Richard Henry Dana's **Two Years Before the Mast** are probably the classics of this genre.

Sailing the Pacific: A Voyage Across the Longest Stretch of Water on Earth, and a Journey into Its Past by Miles Hordern, who sailed there and back from New Zealand to Chile in his twenty-eight-foot sailboat

Sea, Ice, and Rock: Sailing and Climbing Above the Arctic Circle by Chris Bonington and Robin Knox-Johnston gives you two adventures for the price of one.

Sailing buffs won't want to miss **Seamanship: A Voyage Along the Wild Coasts of the British Isles** by Adam Nicolson.

Ten Hours Until Dawn: The True Story of Heroism and Tragedy Aboard the _Can Do_ by Michael Tougias is a **Perfect Storm** read-alike, written well before Junger's book.

In **The Water In Between: A Journey at Sea**, Kevin Patterson—brokenhearted and inexperienced with sailboats—decides to escape his life by sailing from Vancouver to Tahiti. Luckily, he recruits a partner who is sailing savvy (and also brokenhearted).

And for fiction, don't miss the novels by Herman Melville (no need to give titles here, I suspect), Patrick O'Brien, Alexander Kent, Dudley Pope, and C. S. Forester. Others include Herman Wouk's **The Caine Mutiny**, which is a wonderful novel sadly overshadowed by the—it cannot be denied—excellent film, and the novels of Sam Llewellyn, who is to sailing mysteries what Dick Francis is to horse-racing thrillers.

Colin Thubron's **In Siberia** allows readers to accompany the author on his journey across this enormous and enormously mysterious land, from Mongolia to the Arctic Circle, via car, boat, train, bus, and on foot. He takes us to the town where Rasputin was born, the place where the Czar and his family were brutally murdered, and the old Russian prison camps in the Gulag, as well as to museums, private homes, old hotels, and schools. Reading it is a good way to understand Russia after the fall of communism.

In **With Dance Shoes in Siberian Snows**, Sandra Kalniete recalls a life that encompassed growing up in Siberia as the daughter of political prisoners, being allowed at last to move back to Latvia, becoming Latvia's Minister of Foreign Affairs in 2002, and then, in 2004, being appointed the first Latvian Commissioner of the European Union. It's a memoir that makes everything seem possible.

There's a great section in Canadian Colin Angus's **Beyond the Horizon** about experiencing Siberia by bicycle. I have to confess that when I first saw the cover, I thought I had somehow picked up the wrong book. It looked so much like a science fiction novel, and reading the small print on the jacket—"A gripping story of danger, betrayal, and triumph"—confirmed that suspicion. Then I stared at the cover a little longer, shook my head in wonder, opened the book and started reading, and discovered an amazing (true) story. Angus, an experienced outdoor adventurer, decided to do what no one had done before (although a bit of Googling revealed that two other men were attempting it as well): he was determined to circle the world using human power alone. Here's how he describes the plan that he and his travel partner, Tim Harvey, came up with:

We would start on bicycle, heading north from
Vancouver to Fairbanks, Alaska, where the roads
ended. We would continue by rowboat down the
Yukon River and then 400 kilometers (250 miles)
across the Bering Sea to Siberia. We would trek
or ski 3,000 kilometers (1,900 miles) of subarctic
steppe until we hit the far eastern limit of the
European road system, which, again on bicycle, we
would follow westward to Portugal. From there,
we would row across the Atlantic Ocean to North
American shores, and then cycle the final leg back
to Vancouver. We hoped to complete the 42,000
kilometers (26,000 miles) in less than two years.

Naturally, nothing went smoothly, from a kidney infection that
required Angus to abandon the trip and fly home to Canada for
surgery, to interpersonal issues that caused him to end his travels
with Harvey, as well as financial difficulties, and, of course, weather
at sea and on land. And the cover image turned out to be Angus,
dressed for his Siberian trek.

When she was in her seventies, Dervla Murphy forsook long
bike journeys to take a slow train through Siberia, from Moscow to
Vladivostok, which she describes in **Silverland: A Winter Journey
Beyond the Urals**. This was actually her second trip there; her first
was recorded in **Through Siberia by Accident**.

Other Siberian true tales include these: Benson Bobrick's **East of
the Sun: The Epic Conquest and Tragic History of Siberia**
(probably the best history you'll find); Ian Frazier's **Travels in
Siberia**; Mark Jenkins's **Off the Map: Bicycling Across
Siberia**; George Kennan's **Tent Life in Siberia: An Incredible Account of Siberian Adventure, Travel, and Survival**

(originally written in the 1860s and still a breathtaking read); Nikolai Maslov's **Siberia** (a graphic novel); Peter Matthiessen's **Baikal: Sacred Sea of Siberia** (with photographs by Boyd Norton); Jeffrey Tayler's **River of No Reprieve: Descending Siberia's Waterway of Exile, Death, and Destiny**; Peter Thomson's **Sacred Sea: A Journey to Lake Baikal** (former NPR environmental reporter quits job and travels to the other side of the world); and Piers Vitebsky's **The Reindeer People: Living with Animals and Spirits in Siberia**.

As for fiction, try these:

Amy Bloom's **Away**; Lionel Davidson's **Kolymsky Heights**; Fyodor Dostoyevsky's **The House of the Dead** (obviously one of the less well-known novels by the great Russian writer but still necessary reading for fans); Clair Huffaker's **The Cowboy and the Cossack** (if there is only one out of print book that should be reissued by some publisher, somewhere, it would be this brilliant novel); Stuart Kaminsky's **A Cold Red Sunrise**, **Murder on the Trans-Siberian Express**, and **People Who Walk in Darkness** are novels of a long-running series featuring one-legged Russian policeman Porfiry Petrovich Rostnikov—in these outings, the good cop is dispatched to Siberia to uncover some evil doings; James Meek's **The People's Act of Love**; Martin Cruz Smith's **Polar Star** (one of the series that began with **Gorky Park**); and Alexander Solzhenitsyn's **One Day in the Life of Ivan Denisovich**.

SICILY

If you are wondering where to spend a vacation, you will have no doubts as to the benefits of flying to Sicily immediately after reading **Sicilian Odyssey** by Francine Prose. She describes—in luminous prose—just how important the country was in myth, legend, and history. I hadn't known, for example, that Daedalus, after watching his son Icarus fly too near the sun and thus have his wax wings melted, retired to Sicily to nurse his sorrow at the death of his son.

Other nonfiction about Sicily includes Norman Lewis's classic **In Sicily**; **Midnight in Sicily** by Peter Robb; Matthew Fort's **Sweet Honey, Bitter Lemons** (a particularly good choice for foodies); and for travelers interested in the history of a region, Nancy Goldstone's totally readable **The Lady Queen: The Notorious Reign of Joanna I, Queen of Naples, Jerusalem, and Sicily**.

Probably the classic Sicilian novel is **The Leopard** by Giuseppe di Lampedusa, although when it was first written in 1988, it was deemed unpublishable. Set in 1860, when the unification of Italy was underway, the novel is the story of an astronomer who watches the dissolution of his world with the emotional distance of a scientist charting the night sky. The translation by Archibald Colquhoun is splendid. One of the most quoted lines from the novel (which I've found applicable to all sorts of situations) is, "If we want things to stay as they are, things will have to change."

Other novels set in Sicily include Andrea Camilleri's **The Shape of Water**, the first of a mystery series featuring Police Inspector Salvo Montalbano, each one marked by a series of eccentric characters and a tangible sense of the country (at my last count, there were ten novels in the series—the most recent is **The Wings of the Sphinx**); Leonardo Sciascia's **The Wine-Dark Sea**; Mary Taylor Simeti's **On Persephone's Island: A Sicilian Journal**; and **The Almond Picker** by Simonetta Agnello Hornby. One of the most amusing novels set here is **Sicilian Tragedee**, a loose—on many levels—retelling of Romeo and Juliet by Ottavio Cappellani, with a fine colloquial translation by Frederika Randall.

SO WE/I BOUGHT (OR BUILT) A HOUSE IN . . .

I don't know anyone who at one time or another hasn't dreamed of chucking it all: leaving, say, Ithaca, Tulsa, Ann Arbor, or Bozeman; and making a new life, with a new house, in, for example, rural France, Italy, England, Ireland, Spain, or Greece. Or acquiring a yurt in a small but charming Tibetan village. It doesn't really matter where as long as it's Away. And anywhere that you might want to hang your hat, there's a good chance someone has already been there, done that, and met all the quirky neighbors.

So if you're dreaming about decamping and relocating, try these:

> It seems as though many people who visit Morocco end up falling in love with it and moving there. Australian Suzanna Clarke and her husband bought a *riad* (a traditional Moroccan house, with a garden in the middle) in Fez (aka Fes-el-Bali), a walled medieval city. The city itself is much less touristy than Rabat,

Tangier, or Marrakesh, and for ecotourists it's totally car free. It's hard not to want to duplicate the Clarkes' experiences by uprooting yourself and moving as close to them as possible; you can get reasonably close by reading **A House in Fez: Building a Life in the Ancient Heart of Morocco**.

Tony Cohan's **On Mexican Time: A New Life in San Miguel**

Judy Corbett's **Castles in the Air: The Restoration Adventures of Two Young Optimists and a Crumbling Old Mansion**

Betsy Draine and Michael Hinden's **A Castle in the Backyard: The Dream of a House in France** (the Perígord, in the Dordogne valley in Southwest France)

Sally Gable's **Palladian Days: Finding a New Life in a Venetian Country House** (What's it like to live in a villa designed by famed Renaissance architect Andrea Palladio? Gable tells all. Or nearly.)

Barry Golson's **Gringos in Paradise: An American Couple Builds Their Retirement Dream House in a Seaside Village in Mexico** (The title precludes any annotation I might make.)

Martin Kirby's **No Going Back: Journey to Mother's Garden** tells the story of his family (him, his wife, and two very small kids) moving from England to a farmhouse in Northern Spain.

Binka Le Breton's **Where the Road Ends: A Home in the Brazilian Rainforest** describes how she and her husband left their successful lives in Washington, D.C., to move to South America and embrace a new dream.

Beverley Nichols's **Merry Hall**, **Laughter on the Stairs**, and **Sunlight on the Lawn** are only three of his charming books about redoing the house and gardens of several different homes in the British countryside.

Tahir Shah's **The Caliph's House** describes the house his family bought in Morocco, which happened to have a most distinguished history (although it was, in the style of the genre, not in great shape when they bought it).

Niall Williams and Christine Breen's **O Come Ye Back to Ireland** (followed by **When Summer's in the Meadow** and **The Pipes Are Calling**) depicts life in County Clare.

SOJOURNS IN SOUTH ASIA

It may not be politically astute (or correct) to link India and Pakistan in one category, but I'm counting on readers to forgive me for doing so.

For a readable yet authoritative account of the founding of Pakistan and its terrible aftermath, read Yasmin Khan's **The Great Partition: The Making of India and Pakistan**.

Probably the most popular book in the last decade about this area is Greg Mortenson's **Three Cups of Tea: One Man's Mission to Fight Terrorism and Build Nations . . . One School at a Time**. The sequel, equally worth your attention, is **Stones**

into Schools: Promoting Peace with Books, Not Bombs, in Afghanistan and Pakistan.

India

The Opium Wars of the 1830s are the backdrop for Amitav Ghosh's vivid and moving **Sea of Poppies**, which is filled with three-dimensional characters (including Calcutta); it manages the novelistic feat of showing the depredations of colonialism without coming right out and saying it.

> Justine Hardy's **In the Valley of Mist: Kashmir: One Family in a Changing World** takes place against a backdrop of Calcutta and a sea voyage.

> John Keay's **The Great Arc: The Dramatic Tale of How India Was Mapped and Everest Was Named** is dramatic indeed.

> Sudha Koul's **The Tiger Ladies: A Memoir of Kashmir**

> Norman Lewis's **A Goddess in the Stones: Travels in India** was published in 1991, but still opens the country up to readers.

> Octavio Paz's **In Light of India** is a wide-ranging collection of essays based on Paz's years spent with the Mexican Embassy there.

> Basharat Peer's **Curfewed Night** is a memoir of growing up in 1980s Kashmir, and an inside look at the war between India and Pakistan and Hindus and Muslims that raged throughout the 1990s.

Condé Nast Traveler named Ilija Trojanow's **Along the Ganges** as one of the all-time top travel books; you'll understand why when you read it. I felt as though I were there with the author as he makes his way down India's greatest river.

Indian fiction includes Tarquin Hall's **The Case of the Missing Servant**—the first book in a series featuring Vish Puri, "India's Most Private Investigator"—and the second book, **The Man Who Died Laughing**; Aravind Adiga's **The White Tiger** (winner of the Man Booker Prize) and his collection of stories called **Between the Assassinations**; **Six Suspects**, a most unusual mystery by Vikas Swarup (author of **Slumdog Millionaire**, which was made into an Oscar-winning film); Vikram Chandra's **Sacred Games**; Jaspreet Singh's debut novel, **Chef**.

Pakistan

Azhar Abidi's **The House of Bilqis**

Ali Eteraz's **Children of Dust: A Memoir of Pakistan**

Michael Gruber's **The Good Son**, a riveting thriller

Mohammed Hanif's **A Case of Exploding Mangoes** offers a frenetic, frantic, satirical (and fictional) examination of a momentous event in Pakistani history (the violent death of Pakistan's leader, General Zia, and several of his closest associates in 1988).

Daniyal Mueenuddin's **In Other Rooms, Other Wonders** showcases the talent of one of Pakistan's leading young writers.

Nicholas Schmidle's **To Live or to Perish Forever: Two Tumultuous Years in Pakistan** is a journalist's account of his stay in this frightening and beautiful country.

Ali Sethi's **The Wish Maker** is a coming-of-age novel set in Lahore in the 1990s.

Kamila Shamsie's novels **Kartography** and **Burnt Shadows**

SOUTH AFRICA

For some reason that I can't quite explain, South Africa has always fascinated me. It might be because one of the first "grown-up" books I remember taking off my parents' bookshelves was **Cry, the Beloved Country**, Alan Paton's classic novel set in Johannesburg in the 1940s. It was the first book I read that explored the life of black South Africans (though Paton himself was white). I've always felt that it's one of those books that everyone ought to read, and certainly it's a great choice for book groups.

I've never lost my interest in South Africa and its painful history, and I am always eager to see how contemporary writers deal with the many scars of its past. So here are some other excellent selections—fiction and nonfiction, thrillers and literary novels—in which South Africa and/or its history comes to vivid life.

Fiction

Malla Nunn's moving **A Beautiful Place to Die** introduces Detective Sergeant Emmanuel Cooper, who returns to South Africa in 1952 following his service in World War II and has to negotiate the racial laws, the Special Branch of the police, and his own memories in trying to solve the murder of an Afrikaner police officer.

It seems as though thrillers are totally transferrable from one country to the next—the plots of Lee Child's sterling series starring Jack Reacher could probably take place without too many (or significant) changes to almost any country in the world. But most South African thrillers depend on their plots (or subtexts of their plots) taking place in a country where history's wounds have never quite healed over. So I can't imagine that Deon Meyer's **Blood Safari**, fast-paced and emotionally nuanced, could be set anywhere else but South Africa.

Achmat Dangor's **Bitter Fruit** is aptly named. It's a chilling novel set during the post-apartheid period, told from the point of the view of a black attorney.

Another novel set during post-apartheid times that reflects the hold of the past on the present is Damon Galgut's **The Good Doctor**.

Zakes Mda's **Ways of Dying** is about Toloki, who ekes out a meager living as a professional mourner in South Africa. It's a novel that describes a difficult life in a place that's filled with violence, and Toloki is a character you won't soon forget.

For me, the most fascinating sections of Richard Mason's novel **Natural Elements** are the ones about the events of the Boer War, presented from a Boer family's point of view. It's a perspective that's often hard to find in historical fiction—indeed, I've never read another novel in which the Boers come off so sympathetically.

White South African writers you won't want to miss are Nadine Gordimer (**July's People** is a good one to start with); Christopher Hope (one of the few novels that can be considered even a tiny bit lighthearted is his satire **Darkest England**, and even that is pretty dark satire); the Nobel Prize–winning J. M. Coetzee (I'd begin my reading with **Disgrace**); André Brink's **A Dry White Season**; and Lynn Freed's **The Servant's Quarters**.

And for anyone who likes unrelentingly depressing books—and you know who you are—try Roger Smith's **Wake Up Dead**.

Nonfiction

The never-say-die traveler-by-two-wheels Dervla Murphy wrote of her six-thousand-mile solo bicycle odyssey—undertaken when she was in her early sixties—through the nine provinces that comprise the new South Africa, documenting its ups and downs (many downs, it must be said), in **South from the Limpopo**.

Martin Meredith's **Diamonds, Gold, and War: The British, the Boers, and the Making of South Africa** is an excellent (and very readable) introduction to the complex relationships between the Boers (descendants of the original Dutch settlers in the Cape) and the British, which heated up exponentially as precious metals such as gold and diamonds were discovered in the area.

For more recent history—set during the exciting and hope-generating post-apartheid era and the election of Nelson Mandela as president of South Africa—take a look at **Bring Me My Machine Gun** by Alec Russell, the world news editor of the *Financial Times*.

Worthy reading can be found in the many memoirs set during the long years of apartheid and after, written by both black and white South Africans. Two of the best are Mark Mathabane's **Kaffir Boy** and Rian Malan's **My Traitor's Heart**.

SPAIN

I feel as though I have a special connection to Spain, even though I've never traveled there. My father, when he was in his twenties, went to Spain to join the fight against Franco and fascism in the Spanish Civil War in 1936. So I grew up hearing about his trek across the Pyrenees Mountains to get to Spain from France, tales of lost causes, and stories of the war itself. My father believed that going to fight in Spain was the best thing he had ever done in his life. The veterans of that war are mostly dead now, but as you'll see from many of the books listed here, though the war ended over sixty years ago, it still lingers in the hearts and minds of Spaniards, no matter which side of the conflict their families fought on.

I'm not sure quite where in *Book Lust To Go* **Journey to the Frontier: Two Roads to the Spanish Civil War** belongs. But this dual biography of Julian Bell (nephew of Virginia Woolf) and John Cornford (grandson of Charles Darwin) by William Abrahams and Peter Stansky is so engaging and so redolent of the atmosphere of the 1930s that I had to put it somewhere. In telling the story of these two young men, Abrahams and Stansky also help explain what motivated so many other young men (and women) to leave their everyday lives behind and join the fight against Franco.

The area known as Galicia is the setting of **Everything but the Squeal: Eating the Whole Hog in Northern Spain** by John Barlow. This mouthwatering book is about both the food and cultural delights of the region.

Spain in Mind: An Anthology is edited by Alice Leccese Powers, who also wrote a useful general introduction and brief bios that introduce each author. It includes shortish essays, fiction, and poetry by an eclectic array of writers, including Somerset Maugham, Andrew Marvell, Langston Hughes, Ernest Hemingway, Washington Irving, Rose Macaulay, and many more.

In **Ghosts of Spain: Travels Through Spain and Its Silent Past**, Giles Tremlett reflects on how Spain's turbulent history is still reverberating (loudly) in the present.

Victoria Hislop's **The Return** is the story of one family's complex involvement in the Spanish Civil War. I've always felt that fiction is a perfect (and painless) way to learn history—and Hislop's novel serves to prove my point.

Although Javier Marías is a Spanish writer, several of his best novels take place in Oxford, England (and many of the characters do have a Spanish background). The elegance of his writing (ably translated by Margaret Jull Costa) is a delight. I would begin my reading of Marías with his most ambitious work yet: a trilogy called **Your Face Tomorrow**, which includes **Fever and Spear**; **Dance and Dream**; and **Poison, Shadow and Farewell**. They need to be read in this order to be best appreciated.

Other books to try include Richard Wright's nonfiction **Pagan Spain**, which was originally published in 1957 and only recently reprinted; Bernard Atxaga's novel **The Accordionist's Son**; **Roads to Santiago: Detours and Riddles in the Lands and History of Spain** by Cees Nooteboom; **Spanish Recognitions: The Roads to the Present** by Mary Lee Settle (about a journey she took there when she was eighty-two); **It's Not About the Tapas: A Spanish Adventure on Two Wheels** by Polly Evans; Laurie Lee's **As I Walked Out One Midsummer Morning** and **A Moment of War: A Memoir of the Spanish Civil War**; Norman Lewis's **The Tomb in Seville**, about a trip to Spain just before the Civil War erupted; Tim Moore's **Travels with My Donkey: One Man and His Ass on a Pilgrimage to Santiago** (love that title); James Michener's **Iberia: Spanish Travels and Reflections**; and Carlos Ruiz Zafón's novel **The Shadow of the Wind**, which offers a vivid picture of 1950s Barcelona.

Thriller fans will want to check out **Winter in Madrid** by C. J. Sansom and the four mysteries by Robert Wilson that are all set in Seville, starring Inspector Javier Falcón. They include, in order, **The Blind Man of Seville**, **The Vanished Hands**, **The Hidden Assassins**, and **The Ignorance of Blood**. Wilson is also the author of many other thrillers, including one set in Spain's neighbor, Portugal: **A Small Death in Lisbon**. Manuel Vázquez Montalbán's mysteries normally take place in Barcelona, but his private detective, Pepe Carvalho, takes a working trip to Argentina in **The Buenos Aires Quintet**.

STAR TREKKERS

A trek can be undertaken by foot, by boat, by cars, by skis, or (as we know from movies and television) by space ship, as well as by any other form of transportation. Here are my favorite accounts of untiring, unstoppable trekkers: these are the writers whose books—no matter their topic—are well worth seeking out. Some are more difficult to track down than others, although I was pleasantly surprised that many were readily available at the library, used bookstore, or via the Internet.

I especially wanted to bring Gavin Young (1928–2001) to the attention of readers, since his books are a bit hard to find and they're so terrific. Young was a British war correspondent and travel writer. His accounts of wandering the world via ships of all sizes, sorts, and shapes include **Slow Boats to China**, which was published in 1981, and its sequel, **Slow Boats Home**, which came out in 1985. They're rich in detail, filled with accounts of the people he meets and the places he visits. They're the kind of books that make you wish you lived in a time when this kind of travel was still possible (it was even difficult for Young to achieve)—although I'm not sure I could handle with such aplomb the travel delays and the fleas, not to mention the pirates.

And then there's Sir Richard Burton, who had such an amazing and peripatetic life—indeed, one could almost use the adjective "unbelievable" to describe it. Edward Rice's biography **Captain Sir Richard Francis Burton** has a subtitle that sums it up rather nicely, I think: *The Secret Agent Who Made the Pilgrimage to Mecca, Discovered the* Kama Sutra*, and Brought the* Arabian Nights *to the West.* If you'd rather read a novel about this fascinating man, try **The Collector of Worlds: A Novel of Sir Richard Francis Burton** by Iliya Troyanov.

Other star trekkers (in alphabetical order) whose books I recommend without reservation include Gertrude Bell, Isabella Bird, Ian Buruma, Robert Byron, Bruce Chatwin, William Dalrymple, Patrick Leigh Fermor, Peter Fleming, Paul Fussell, Tony Horwitz, Pico Iyer, Ryszard Kapuściński, Alexander William Kinglake, Mary Kingsley, Laurie Lee, Norman Lewis, Jan Morris, Dervla Murphy, Eric Newby, Redmond O'Hanlon, Jonathan Raban, Freya Stark, Paul Theroux, and Sara Wheeler.

SWEDE(N), ISN'T IT?

Another Scandinavian country heard from: here you'll find the sort of moody mysteries that give you a dark but effective feel for the country, fictional histories of major events, and accounts of Sweden's role in World War II. What was interesting to me as I was doing all my reading about Sweden is that so many of the books that have been translated into English are for children—Selma Lagerlöf, for example, whose **The Wonderful Adventures of Nils** is much easier to find than are her novels for adults.

Probably the two most popular Swedish writers these days are Henning Mankell and Stieg Larsson. Mankell is best known for his bleak psychological thrillers, many featuring Kurt Wallander, his main character in a series of police procedurals. A good introduction to that aspect of Mankell's oeuvre—and a youngish Wallander—is **The Pyramid: And Four Other Kurt Wallander Mysteries**.

Non-Wallander novels by Mankell include, but aren't limited to, **The Man from Beijing**, **Kennedy's Brain**, **The Return of the Dancing Master** (my favorite), and **Italian Shoes**.

Larsson's first novel of the Millennium Trilogy, **The Girl with the Dragon Tattoo**, was an immediate best seller; he followed it up with **The Girl Who Played with Fire** and **The Girl Who Kicked the Hornet's Nest**. For his gazillion fans (and his family), it was a sad day when he died much too young right after finishing the last book of the three.

(Both Larsson and Mankell are too dark for me to read comfortably, but I am in the tiniest minority, so try them out for yourself.)

Other crime novels to read include Johan Theorin's **Echoes from the Dead**; **Under the Snow** by Kerstin Ekman (as well as her non-mystery novel, **God's Mercy**); Helene Tursten's **Detective Inspector Huss**; **The Princess of Burundi** (and others showcasing Uppsala homicide detective Ann Lindell and her colleagues on the force) by Kjell Eriksson; Åsa Larsson's **Sun Storm** (which won Sweden's Best First Crime Novel Award), **The Blood Spilt**, and others; and **Sun and Shadow** (and others) by Åke Edwardson.

For non-mystery fans who still want to get a sense of Sweden, try **Lewi's Journey** by Per Olov Enquist, translated by the talented

Tiina Nunnally. The ostensible subject—the founding of the Swedish Pentecostal movement—provides the framework for an examination of character, place, and Sweden in the twentieth century. (His other novels, all with a historical framework, take place in other countries: **The Book About Blanche and Marie** in France, and **The Royal Physician's Visit** in Denmark). Others not to miss include **Popular Music from Vittula** by Mikael Niemi (Sweden in the 1960s); **Benny and Shrimp** by Katarina Mazetti; and **Astrid and Veronika** and **Sonata for Miriam** by Linda Olsson.

TEXAS TWO-STEP
(AFTER A BOB WILLS SONG)

I asked Jake Silverstein, the editor of *Texas Monthly*, what books set in Texas, or by Texas authors, are must-reads for anyone planning a real or virtual visit to the state. Partly I figured that if anyone would know the best ones to suggest it would be Jake, and I also wanted to see how many of his suggestions corresponded to ones that I had already read and knew I wanted to include. I'm pleased to say that there was some overlap, but I added many books to my own must-read list, and—after reading them—heartily concur with Jake's choices. Here they are, with Jake's original comments in quotes.

Black Water Rising by Attica Locke: "This thriller is set in Houston in the early 1980s, and deals with race and class issues."

Brownsville by Oscar Casares: "Short stories. Vivid and lucid portrait of being lower-middle class/poor and relatively isolated in Brownsville, Texas."

Friday Night Lights by H. G. Bissinger: "Takes place in Midland/Odessa. High school football. Great nonfiction writing." (And the television adaptation is pretty wonderful as well.)

The Gay Place by Billy Lee Brammer: "Sort of Texas's **All the King's Men**."

George Washington Gómez by Américo Paredes: "Set in 1914 in Texas along the U.S.–Mexico border. Many of the issues raised in the book are, alas, still issues. Also, his incredible book of folklore/history/musicology **With His Pistol in His Hand**, one of the best nonfiction books about Texas you'll ever read."

Horseman, Pass By and **The Last Picture Show** by Larry McMurtry, followed by his slim book of essays about Texas, **In a Narrow Grave**: "Reading this trio gives you a perfect sense of the transition from small towns to cities. And then there's **Lonesome Dove**, of course, which is amazing." I would also add my three favorite McMurtry novels: **Moving On**; its sort-of sequel, **Terms of Endearment**; and **All My Friends Are Going to Be Strangers**.

The Last Known Residence of Mickey Acuña by Dagoberto Gilb: "Set in the area in and around El Paso. Great Tex-Mex voice that slides between English and Spanish. Gilb is one of the best writers in Texas today."

Strange Peaches by Edwin Shrake: "For a sense of Dallas in the early 1960s around the time of the JFK assassination. Eye-opening."

The Time It Never Rained by Elmer Kelton: "Classic portrait of ranching life in the southern plains. Not the old-timey stuff of cowboys and trail drives, but the real deal: struggling to pay bills and keep things going through the terrible drought of the 1950s. Kelton was the son of a ranch foreman and an agricultural reporter for the *San Angelo Standard-Times* for forty years."

Waterloo by Karen Olsson: "For a picture of modern-day Austin."

I'd also add that for a picture of frontier Texas in the last years of the Civil War, you don't want to miss Paulette Jiles's **The Color of Lightning**.

Incidentally, Jake was clearly too modest to mention his own book, set in the southwest (especially Texas and Mexico), **Nothing Happened and Then It Did**. It's set in the present, and melds fiction and nonfiction so cleverly that it's impossible to really be certain which is which. I'll be interested to see where libraries and bookstores decide to shelve it: a novel or not?

THAI TALES

I have to be honest and say that I really have no great desire to spend time in Thailand. What's a bit odd about this fact is that several of my favorite thriller writers—John Burdett and Christopher G. Moore among them—happen to set their books there. On the other hand, the picture of Thailand (especially Bangkok) that these authors present is hyper-violent and utterly grungy. But gosh, for some reason that I really don't care to explore, I really enjoy reading them, at least until they cross over that invisible line in my mind and the violence and grunge become more than I bear.

So if you like your suspense novels set in exotic locales; if you enjoy a sympathetic, all-too-human protagonist; and (this especially) if you don't mind (or have a high tolerance for) grisly and gruesome crimes, you won't want to miss John Burdett's series beginning with **Bangkok 8** and **Bangkok Tattoo**. Thai police detective Sonchai Jitpleecheep stars in these fast-moving more-or-less mysteries that are distinguished by smart (frequently witty) dialogue, a terrific depiction of place, and plot twists galore. The first involves jade smuggling, sexually deviant behavior, and death by snake venom, while the second features the ghastly murder of a CIA agent; both crimes send Sonchai (who struggles to reconcile his Buddhist beliefs with his knowledge of humanity at its worst) deep into the criminal and sexual underworld of Thailand's biggest city. I was totally won over by the character of Sonchai as well as Burdett's smooth writing.

The protagonist of Christopher G. Moore's series is Vincent Calvino, a disbarred American lawyer who sells his services as a private investigator in Bangkok. Start with **Spirit House**, and work forward from there. Moore himself has lived in Bangkok for two decades or so, and the descriptions of the city are themselves worth the price of the book. Oh yes, and the plots are utterly compelling.

Since the first-person narrator in Mischa Berlinski's **Fieldwork** is named Mischa Berlinski, readers might be forgiven for thinking that it's actually a memoir about the author's experiences living in Thailand. That you come away from the book feeling like you've learned a lot compounds that belief. But it is definitely a novel—and an absorbing one, at that. When his girlfriend gets a job teaching in northern Thailand, Mischa decides to go with her, spending his time (and earning a meager living) freelancing for an English-language newspaper. He hears from an old friend and fellow ex-pat about Martiya van der Leun, an American anthropologist who's committed suicide in a Thai prison where she was serving a life sentence for murder. Mischa's interest (soon an obsession) in the mystery surrounding Martiya's life and death leads him to the Walker family, three generations of missionaries working to convert the Thai hill tribes to Christianity, and to the Diyalos, the hill tribe that was the subject of Martiya's PhD dissertation. For me, the novel worked on three levels. First, it's a wonderfully written, satisfyingly complex why-dunit, as we follow Mischa in his attempt to understand why Martiya ended up in prison. Second, it's a great character-driven novel, as Berlinski offers sympathetic portrayals of both the Walkers and the tribespeople they love, and whose souls they want to save for Jesus. The Diyalos in particular, although they are entirely a figment of Berlinski's (the author's, not the character's) imagination, are presented so vividly that their customs, beliefs, and way of life seem quite real. Third, the novel is, despite Martiya's ultimate fate, a tribute to anthropologists and the work they do. Reading **Fieldwork** made me wish I had taken more anthropology courses in college, and finishing it sent me to the library in search of many of the books mentioned in Berlinski's notes on the sources for the novel.

Other works of fiction set in Thailand include Alex Garland's **The Beach**; Lily Tuck's **Siam, Or the Woman Who Shot a Man**; Dorothy Gilman's **Mrs. Pollifax and the Golden Triangle**;

Rattawut Lapcharoensap's collection **Sightseeing: Stories**; and **A Nail Through the Heart**, the first of the Bangkok-set Poke Rafferty thrillers by Timothy Hallinan.

If you're interested in non-fiction, try Karen Connelly's **Dream of a Thousand Lives: A Sojourn in Thailand**, which won Canada's Governor General's Literary Award.

TIMBUKTU AND BEYOND

I have a friend who went to Mali solely, she tells me, so she could tell people that she'd been to Timbuktu. She had a glorious time and I envy her adventurous nature a lot. Here are some excellent accounts of other travelers exploring that fabled land.

One of my favorite passages from Mark Jenkins's **To Timbuktu: A Journey Down the Niger** is this:

> Strange things happen in Africa. Fantastic things. Things you can't understand. You sense they portend something but you don't know what. Africans are accustomed to it. For them strangeness is commonplace. They don't try to decipher it. If they have a problem, they talk to a lawyer or an accountant or a shaman or a necromancer. Depends on the problem.

I love the matter-of-factness of it—the need, when you're traveling, to take whatever you see, hear, or experience, without judgment. In recounting his attempt to discover the source of the Niger River and follow it into Mali, Jenkins, as he always does in his travel books, takes us along on the journey. (A good selection of his other travel writings can be found in **A Man's Life: Dispatches from Dangerous Places**.)

Another good read about a river journey to Timbuktu is Kira Salak's **The Cruelest Journey: Six Hundred Miles to Timbuktu**.

Marq de Villiers and Sheila Hirtle have written a fascinating book about the history and culture of Mali's famed city in **Timbuktu: The Sahara's Fabled City of Gold**. As the authors point out, one of the city's treasures is a collection of four thousand manuscripts in the Mamma Haidara Library, brought together and preserved by the leading families of the region and which offer their readers an invaluable look into the region's past (some date back to the thirteenth century).

Kris Holloway's **Monique and the Mango Rains: Two Years with a Midwife in Mali**, which describes the author's experiences as a Peace Corps volunteer in a remote village, made me think about many issues—women's lives in nonindustrialized countries, health care in the poorest areas of the world, and the human connections that cross age, ethnicity, and backgrounds. Rather inspiring, actually.

TO THE ENDS OF THE EARTH: NORTH AND SOUTH

I f I were going to the Arctic or Antarctic, the book I'd pick up first is **The Ends of the Earth: The Arctic: An Anthology of the Finest Writing on the North Pole**, edited by Elizabeth Kolbert, which is bound with **The Ends of the Earth: The Antarctic: An Anthology of the Finest Writing on the South Pole**, edited by Francis Spufford. Here's where you can get a taste of what you might want to read next, which I hope will include some of these fascinating books.

The Arctic

The Last Gentleman Adventurer: Coming of Age in the Arctic by Edward Beauclerk Maurice is the charming tale of a young man who apprenticed with the Hudson's Bay Company in 1930 and stayed on because he fell in love with living so far from civilization.

Martin Frobisher, the fascinating main subject of **Unknown Shore: The Lost History of England's Arctic Colony** by Robert Ruby, was a complicated individual—part pirate and part adventurer. He led three failed expeditions to locate the famed Northwest Passage in order to set up a British colony for Queen Elizabeth I. Frobisher's story is less well known than most of the other Northwest Passage seekers, and that we know it at all is probably due to the second subject of Ruby's book, the American Charles Francis Hall, who in 1860 traveled to the Arctic to do a series of oral histories with Inuits. Ruby does a wonderful job of showing us what those sixteenth-century explorers were up against: "Geography, like a distant lover, changed according to expectations and desires. . . . Every few years cartographers refashioned their maps."

Only the most dedicated and determined fans of Arctic exploration will know of John Rae, but after reading Ken McGoogan's skillfully written **Fatal Passage: The Story of John Rae, the Arctic Hero Time Forgot**, readers will recognize the important place in history that he deserves. As McGoogan puts it, Rae discovered "the final navigable link in the Northwest Passage, at last connecting the Atlantic and Pacific oceans across the top of North America." But in addition, McGoogan tells us, Rae also solved the mystery of what happened to John Franklin's 1845 Northwest Passage expedition (cannibalism, not to mince words), and his discovery was not much appreciated by Franklin's devoted followers in England. More to the point, it greatly displeased Lady Jane, Franklin's wealthy widow, who brought the immensely popular Charles Dickens into the fray on Franklin's side. This particular angle is deftly explored in Richard Flanagan's novel **Wanting**. Lady Jane Franklin has her own say—and travels—in Ken McGoogan's **Lady Franklin's Revenge: A True Story of Ambition, Obsession, and the Remaking of Arctic History**.

Which brings us to John Franklin himself. His importance in Arctic exploration is unchallenged, though he never succeeded in discovering what he set out to find. **Ice Blink: The Tragic Fate of Sir John Franklin's Lost Polar Expedition** by Scott Cookman is a very readable biography of the man, and your local librarian can probably find you more scholarly tomes to peruse if your interest is piqued by Franklin's life. (He always shows up somewhere in every book about the search for the Northwest Passage, as well. Personally, I've always found it fascinatingly grim that Franklin's two ships were named the *Terror* and *Erebus*. How awfully prescient!) There's a terrific novel by the prolific and multi-talented Dan Simmons that deals with Franklin's expedition called, forebodingly, **The Terror**, and it lives up to its name.

Anthony Brandt's invigorating **The Man Who Ate His Boots: The Tragic History of the Search for the Northwest**

Passage also makes good use of the myths (or truths) that have grown up around the disappearance of Franklin and all his men. It offers a great overview of the whole history of the attempts to find that dang Passage.

To the End of the Earth: Our Epic Journey to the North Pole and the Legend of Peary and Henson by Tom Avery tries to answer one of the major questions of the early twentieth century: Was it really possible that U.S. Naval Commander Robert Peary and his team of dogs got to the North Pole in just thirty-seven days? Avery and his team set out to replicate Peary's journey as closely as possible: part adventure and part history add up to a spellbinding saga.

There are a few writers whose books I always know I'll read—no matter the subject. Fergus Fleming is one of those, and I was especially delighted with **Ninety Degrees North: The Quest for the North Pole**. This outstanding history has something for everyone: questers, dreamers, and a story that can't be beat.

Jennifer Niven's **Ada Blackjack: A True Story of Survival in the Arctic** and **The Ice Master: The Doomed 1913 Voyage of the _Karluk_** are amazing tales—well wrought and filled with captivating characters. They're perfect for fans of Junger and Krakauer.

Other Arctic-related books that would fill the bill for armchair travelers are **Farthest North: The Epic Adventure of a Visionary Explorer** by the late nineteenth–century Arctic voyager and Nobel Prize winner, Norwegian Fridtjof Nansen; **Fatal Journey: The Final Expedition of Henry Hudson** by Peter C. Mancall; and Gretel Ehrlich's **In the Empire of Ice: Life in a Changing Landscape**.

Antarctic

To put it quite simply, I adore Sara Wheeler's books. Her writing is filled with engaging humor, she does her homework before she visits a country, she's fearless (more about that later), and she has the particular kind of luck that serious travelers (or, at least, travel writers) seem to have. They're always meeting up with just the right people at just the right time, in order, for example, to hitch a ride (frequently in planes and helicopters) to an otherwise inaccessible place. And they're always being upgraded to better hotel rooms. (That's only happened to me once.) Wheeler's masterpiece is, I think, **Terra Incognita: Travels in Antarctica**, which is partly an account of her own experiences as part of the American National Science Foundation's Antarctic Artists' and Writers' Program, and partly a history of the exploration of the region. That history is made up of both wise and foolish decisions, luck (both good and bad), heroism, and the inevitable fatalities.

Now for the fearlessness: I have one very adventurous daughter, who, like Wheeler, has an amazing gift for friendship and instant closeness with nearly everyone she meets. At one time in her life she would drop whatever plans she had in order to go off rock climbing with a group of strangers, fax us updates on whatever was happening in her life on stationery from her new boyfriend's place of employment (this particular one was a bodyguard for the president of a Spanish province that shall go unnamed), have her passport confiscated on a train between Florence and Budapest, sleep on the couches of strangers, be out of touch for weeks on end, and generally keep my anxiety level sky high. So, all the time

I was reading Wheeler's wonderful books, I was feeling dreadfully sorry for her mother.

Wheeler is also the author of two great biographies: **Too Close to the Sun: The Audacious Life and Times of Denys Finch Hatton** (you might remember him as Robert Redford in the film *Out of Africa*—he was the lover of both Isak Dinesen and Beryl Markham) and **Cherry: A Life of Apsley Cherry-Garrard** (one of the men who accompanied Robert Falcon Scott on the Terra Nova expedition to the South Pole in 1910–1913).

One writer you'll want to become familiar with is Roland Huntford, but when you read him, keep in mind that he was pretty pro-Amundsen and pretty anti-Scott. Here are the books of his that I'd suggest reading first: **The Last Place on Earth** (originally published in the 1980s as **Scott and Amundsen**), as well as the biography, **Shackleton**.

Stephanie L. Barczewski explores the differing trajectories of the careers and reputations of two major explorers in **Antarctic Destinies: Scott, Shackleton, and the Changing Face of Heroism**.

As part of the Australasian Antarctic Expedition, Douglas Mawson (actually, Sir Douglas Mawson—he was knighted for his work there) spent years traversing the harsh landscape and enduring the frigid weather; he wrote about his experiences in **The Home of the Blizzard: A True Story of Antarctic Survival**. There's also an excellent book about his 1911 trek to the South Pole: Lennard Bickel's **Mawson's Will: The Greatest Polar Survival Story Ever Written**.

TRAVEL TO IMAGINARY PLACES

I don't use the phrase "tour de force" very often (mostly because I'm always nervous that I'll say "tour de France" by accident instead), but the books in this section all qualify for the correct phrase. They are A+ examples of how a vivid but disciplined imagination and splendid writing can combine to produce unforgettably wonderful books. When I read them I wondered if I (as well as the history books and atlases) had somehow missed the existence of these places. The odd thing is that some of these are shelved in the science fiction and fantasy section, while others are considered "literary." Still, no matter where they're shelved, they're all truly amazing—fiction that could almost be nonfiction. Try them and see if you don't agree with me.

Jorge Luis Borges's long short story "Tlön, Uqbar, Orbis Tertius"

Peter Cameron's **Andorra** and **The City of Your Final Destination**

Michael Chabon's **The Yiddish Policemen's Union**

Gabriel García Márquez's **One Hundred Years of Solitude**

Ursula K. Le Guin's **The Wizard of Earthsea**

Stephen Marche's brilliant **Shining at the Bottom of the Sea**

China Miéville's **The City and the City**

Steven Millhauser's **Martin Dressler: The Tale of an American Dreamer**, set in a city that is New York, but not quite the Manhattan we know

Jan Morris's **Hav**, comprised of **Last Letters from Hav**
and **Hav of the Myrmidons**

Adam Thorpe's **Ulverton**

Evelyn Waugh's **Scoop** (It's totally politically incorrect
and rollickingly funny. Don't read it if you're easily
offended by racial or ethnic epithets.)

Colson Whitehead's **The Intuitionist** (I had the
same feeling about this novel as I did about the
Millhauser book.)

TRAVELERS' TALES IN VERSE

I couldn't resist including some of my favorite poems that evoke
in me (and, I hope, you) a sense of journeying, of leaving the
familiar for the unknown.

Constantine Cavafy's "Ithaca" (sometimes spelled "Ithaka")

Walter de la Mare's "The Listeners"

Robert Frost's "The Road Not Taken"

G. K. Chesterton's "Lepants"

Rudyard Kipling's "Mandalay"

John Masefield's "Sea Fever"

Carl Sandburg's "The Road and the End"

Sara Teasdale's "The Long Hill"

W. J. Turner's "Romance"

Henry Van Dyke's "America for Me"

TURKISH DELIGHTS

Turkey is such a prime destination for travelers interested in its history and culture that there is much good fiction and nonfiction that lets us experience the country in all its complexity. Here's an *ortaya karışık* (hodgepodge) of titles for you.

Nonfiction

A Fez of the Heart: Travels Around Turkey in Search of a Hat is author Jeremy Seal's study of Turkish life, customs, and history in context as he attempts to understand the importance of the fez, a maroon felt hat, to Turkish sensibilities. In 1925, two years after Turkey became a republic, the great reformer Mustafa Kemal Ataturk outlawed the wearing of turbans. He made the fez the national hat. With humor, warmth, and great insight, Seal does an excellent job helping western readers understand how precariously placed Turkey is between the past and present, between the mores of Islam and those of Europe.

Tales from the Expat Harem: Foreign Women in Modern Turkey, edited by Anastasia M. Ashman and Jennifer Eaton Gökmen, is a collection of essays that examine Turkish life and traditions from the point of view of thirty-two non-Turkish women who moved there for adventure, work, or love.

Mary Lee Settle spent three years living in Turkey and wrote about her experiences in **Turkish Reflections: A Biography of a Place**, first published in 1991. In addition, an important part of Settle's incandescent novel **Celebration** takes place in a small Turkish town.

Other nonfiction exploring the complex history of this country includes Giles Milton's **Paradise Lost: Smyrna 1922**, about the destruction of a city on the Aegean coast, along with thousands of its citizens, by Turkish troops under the leadership of Ataturk; and Freya Stark's **Alexander's Path: A Travel Memoir**.

Fiction

One of the best novels I've ever read is Louis de Bernières's **Birds Without Wings**, which is set in a small coastal town in Anatolia during the dying days of the Ottoman Empire. It's narrated in dozens of voices, including those of the men and women of town, the rich and the poor, the nobles and peasants, the Christians and Muslims, the Greeks and the Armenians—all ordinary people who have lived together for generations in peace, unnoticed and far from the seats of influence, until they're swept up in the maelstrom of war and become simple pawns of history, subject to the decisions of their misguided, often incompetent, and always dangerously power-hungry rulers. Along with the story of the residents of this one small town, de Bernières tells of the rise of Kemal Ataturk, whose goal was to remake Turkey into a modern, secular country. These parallel tales play off one another brilliantly and together make for a particularly rich and satisfying novel. You can actually go to the ghost town (near Fethiye) where the novel takes place.

Jason Goodwin's fascination with Turkey is evident in his entertaining mystery series set there in the 1830s, all featuring Yashim Togalu, a eunuch and a detective. They include, in order, **The Janissary Tree**, **The Snake Stone**, and **The Bellini Card**. I think you could probably pass many a Turkish history test with what you take in about the country while reading these. Goodwin also wrote **Lords of the Horizons: A History of the Ottoman Empire**, which is both easy to digest and informative.

Three Turkish novelists of note are Nobel Prize–winning Orhan Pamuk, Yashar Kemal, and Elif Shafak. Pamuk's **My Name Is Red** and **The Black Book** are two good ones with which to begin. Set in the 1930s, Kemal's first novel, **Memed, My Hawk**, was published in 1955 and is the beginning of a quartet about a boy coming of age in southern Turkey. Shafak's **The Bastard of Istanbul** and **The Forty Rules of Love: A Novel of Rumi** make for engrossing reading. As for non-Turkish novelists writing about Turkey, try these: Maureen Freely's **Enlightenment**; Barry Unsworth's **The Rage of the Vulture**; Alan Drew's **Gardens of Water**; Peter Ackroyd's **The Fall of Troy**; and **Dervishes** by Beth Helms. If you're looking for something a lot lighter in tone and mood that still gives you a sense of Turkish life and customs, don't miss Dorothy Gilman's **The Amazing Mrs. Pollifax**.

VENI, VIDI, VENICE

From what I can recall, my first introduction to the city of Venice was in **Betsy and the Great World**, one of the Betsy-Tacy series by Maud Hart Lovelace. Since I so strongly identified with Betsy, I felt as though there was no need for me to go since Betsy experienced it all for me. (And she fell in love with the devastatingly handsome Marco, besides, although she never forgot Joe Willard. What can I say, you have to be eleven and read it yourself.)

Over the years I've read other books—both fiction and narrative nonfiction—that did make me want to visit that most unusual of cities. Probably the best book to read about the history of Venice as seen through its art and architecture is Mary McCarthy's **Venice Observed**. Despite its age (it was originally published in 1956), it's still in print and still valuable reading for any trip to the city.

One of the books that explores contemporary Venice, and sketches the city's descent from world-leadership status in the fifteenth century to its (sad to say, relatively) minor place in the world today (that is, minor except in the hearts of Venetians and those who love the city dearly), is John Berendt's **The City of Falling Angels**. He arrived for an extended visit right after the magnificent opera house, La Fenice, was destroyed by fire in 1996. One of the things that struck me about this chatty and appealing book, besides the wonderful descriptions of people from all walks of life whom Berendt meets and talks to, is how beautiful he makes the city sound despite its bureaucratic nightmares and dangers of being overrun by tourists or destroyed by erosion from the Adriatic Sea. Here's a quote I find especially evocative about the lure of Venice:

> To me Venice was not merely beautiful; it was beautiful everywhere. On one occasion I set about testing this notion by concocting a game called "photo roulette," the object of which was to walk around the city taking photographs at unplanned moments—whenever a church bell

rang or at every sighting of a dog or cat—to see how often, standing at an arbitrary spot one would be confronted by a view of exceptional beauty. The answer: almost always.

No plans for a trip to Venice would be complete without reading the series of mysteries by American Donna Leon, all of which feature Commissario Guido Brunetti; the first, published in 1992, is **Death at La Fenice**. One of the pleasures of reading Leon is getting to know Brunetti's family and co-workers, as well as the mouthwatering descriptions of food and drink. (The first time I drank prosecco, the sparkling wine of Italy, was after reading about it in this series.) For walkers (and Brunetti fans) like me, it's fun to dream of replicating the strolls described in **Brunetti's Venice: Walks Through Venice with the City's Best-Loved Detective** by Toni Sepeda (with an introduction by Donna Leon).

Louis Begley and Anka Muhlstein, longtime married, spend two weeks a year writing in Venice. **Venice for Lovers** is an account, in each author's voice, of their passion for the city; in addition, there's a charming novella by Begley about the experience of a young man who falls in love with a place and a person.

And that maven of manners, Judith Martin—Miss Manners herself—is also a Venetophile, as can be seen quite clearly in her **No Vulgar Hotel: The Desire and Pursuit of Venice**.

The best parts of Deborah Weisgall's novel **The World Before Her** describe the experiences of two very different women in Venice. One is a thirty-three-year-old American sculptor named Caroline. The other, sixty-one-year-old Marian Evans, is the very real nineteenth-century English novelist better known by her pen name, George Eliot. Alternating chapters, many set in Venice, move from 1880 (Marian's tale) to 1980 (Caroline's story) and back again.

Experiencing Venice through each of your senses is the goal of native Venetian Tiziano Scarpa's **Venice Is a Fish: A Sensual Guide**.

Other contemporary novels I've enjoyed that take place in that watery wonderland include Kathryn Walker's **A Stopover in Venice**; the fabulous mystery **Thus Was Adonis Murdered** by Sarah Caudwell; and Salley Vickers's **Miss Garnet's Angel**.

Among the many Venetian-set historical novels, you won't want to miss Sarah Dunant's **In the Company of the Courtesan**; the novels of Dorothy Dunnett, in which Venice has a central role—especially, but not exclusively, **Scales of Gold**, part four of the House of Niccolo series; and the third in a series of historical mysteries by Jason Goodwin, **The Bellini Card**. And after reading it (in Venice, preferably) you could stop and have a Bellini in the shadow of the Rialto Bridge, as one of the fans of this book told me she did.

VERONA

Verona's probably best known as the location of two of Shakespeare's plays: *Romeo and Juliet* and *The Two Gentlemen of Verona*. But it turns out that, bookwise at least, it's a swell place to spend a vacation. Tim Parks's **Italian Neighbors: Or a Lapsed Anglo-Saxon in Verona** and **An Italian Education: The Further Adventures of an Expatriate in Verona** are delightful memoirs. Parks also wrote **A Season with Verona: Travels Around**

Italy in Search of Illusion, National Character and . . . Goals!, about his obsession with the Verona soccer team. Those who admire irony with a definite bite will enjoy Parks's novel set in Verona, **Juggling the Stars**.

In his captivating mystery, **Death in Verona**, Roy Harley Lewis takes a fresh (fictional) look at the lives of the characters in Shakespeare's *Romeo and Juliet*, especially Lady Capulet.

VIENNA

Whether it's described in fiction, biography, or history, Vienna has a storied aura about it, as can be readily seen by the books suggested here.

Three histories of Vienna that offer outstanding general background on the country's place in the world order are Carl Schorske's **Fin-de-Siècle Vienna: Politics and Culture**; Frederic Morton's **Thunder at Twilight: Vienna 1913/1914**; and Paul Hofmann's **The Viennese: Splendor, Twilight, and Exile**. All are well worth a read.

Frank Tallis's novels provide almost a contemporary guide to early twentieth-century Vienna, and they're awfully good mysteries, too. Start with **A Death in Vienna**, in which he introduces his protagonists, Detective Oskar Rheinhardt and his good friend, Max Liebermann, a physician and follower of Sigmund Freud. The cases continue in **Vienna Blood**, **Fatal Lies**, and **Vienna Secrets**.

J. Sydney Jones's **The Empty Mirror** is set in the last years of the nineteenth century; the painter Gustav Klimt is a suspect in a series of murders. The (fictional) lawyer Karl Werthen works with the (real) criminologist Hanns Gross to find the killer. It's followed by **Requiem in Vienna**.

Probably the most important novel about pre–World War I Vienna is Robert Musil's **The Man Without Qualities**. Clark Thayer, a friend from Tulsa, suggested that I read this—it was one of his favorite novels. It was a formidably challenging read for me, but I grew to appreciate its modernist intricacies and comic tone. There's a new-ish translation by Sophie Wilkins, which wasn't available when I read Musil's grand novel early in the 1980s. I wish I could tell Clark how much I enjoyed it, but alas, we lost touch years ago.

For a more contemporary picture of the city, try the very weird but wonderful novel—or collection of interlinked and (somewhat) autobiographical stories—**The System of Vienna: From Heaven Street to Earth Mound Square** by Gert Jonke. This is a perfect book for anyone who is interested in playful language and doesn't demand reality from the plots of novels.

Because I love both history and many memoirs, I was quite taken with Marjorie Perloff's memoir **The Vienna Paradox**, in which she looks at pre–World War II Vienna in the light of her family's experiences.

Among all the other famous people that were born or lived in Vienna, the Wittgenstein family is one of the best known. Alexander Waugh's **The House of Wittgenstein: A Family at War** traces the experiences of its ill-fated members.

Other novels with a Viennese setting include Philip Kerr's **A German Requiem**; Graham Greene's **The Third Man** (also a terrific movie, maybe one of the few that's better than the book

Halberstam's **The Best and the Brightest** (don't miss reading this one); James Webb's powerful novel **Fields of Fire**; and **The Lotus Eaters** by Tatjana Soli, which is, quite simply, a spectacularly wonderful novel. I also highly recommended Tim O'Brien's novels set in Vietnam: **The Things They Carried**, **In the Lake of the Woods**, and **Going After Cacciato**.

In addition, Curbstone Press publishes a series called Voices from Vietnam, which brings the works of Vietnamese authors to American readers.

WALES WELCOMES YOU

The book you absolutely must read before journeying to Wales is **How Green Was My Valley** by Richard Llewellyn. The story of Huw Morgan's coming of age in a small Welsh mining town is one of those books that I wish I could read again for the first time—it's the same way I feel about Paul Scott's Raj Quartet, which is set in a totally different part of the world entirely.

And then can you move on to these:

Jan Morris's **A Writer's House in Wales** is distinguished by her keen eye for detail, her fine writing, and her enthusiasm for her subject. It's mostly a memoir, but also includes a good deal of Welsh history and culture packed into a short (168 pages) book.

Judy Corbett and her partner, Peter Welford (a bookbinder and architectural historian), discovered the dilapidated Gwydir Castle in Northern Wales and decided—impulsively—to buy it and restore it to its former glorious state. Corbett writes about their experiences in **Castles in the Air: The Restoration Adventures of Two Young Optimists and a Crumbling Old Mansion**. And there's even a ghost from the seventeenth century. Travelers to Wales can stay at the restored castle, now operating as a B&B.

No book lover will be able to resist the myriad charms of all of Paul Collins's books, and perhaps especially those of **Sixpence House: Lost in a Town of Books**. In it, Collins describes the period in which he; his wife, Jennifer; and his young son, Morgan, lived in Hay-on-Wye, known as the Welsh "town of books." Woven in with the stories of houses they tried to buy and his part-time job in the biggest used bookstore in town are captivating accounts of books Collins discovers, as well as ruminations on book titles, the vagaries of publishing, literary hoaxes, and the fate of many unsung writers through the centuries whose books never made the splash they deserved.

Others not to miss include Horatio Clare's **Running for the Hills: Growing Up on My Mother's Sheep Farm in Wales**, which is both lovely and loving; Bruce Chatwin's **On the Black Hill** (anything by Chatwin is worth reading; this novel is no exception); Kathryn Davis's novel **The Walking Tour**; Tessa Hadley's **The Master Bedroom**; Susan Fletcher's Whitbread Award–winning poetic debut novel, **Eve Green**; and Owen Sheers's **Resistance** (an alternate history centering on a German invasion of the country during World War II—it's an unforgettable novel).

And mystery fans won't want to miss Rhys Bowen's mystery novels featuring Constable Evan Evans. **Evans Above** is the first one, but they don't really need to be read in order. Canadian author Elizabeth J. Duncan sets her cozies in Wales. She won the Malice

Domestic Best First Traditional Mystery competition for **The Cold Light of Mourning**, so begin with that, and then reach for its sequel, **A Brush with Death**.

WALK RIGHT IN

There are WALKERS and then there are walkers. The uppercase variety long to traverse a country by foot, or navigate the Appalachian Trail from Georgia to Maine, or walk from one end of Manhattan to the other. The lowercase walkers, while otherwise certainly eminently honorable and pleasant people, have no such ambitions. They are fine with travel by trains, planes, automobiles, bicycles, horses, and camels. WALKERS feel that ambulating gets them to the heart of a place in the way no other mode of transportation can do. I aspire to join their ranks (although I fear I may have left it too late). I find that walking clears my mind, lifts my spirits, and allows me to see the world from a slower, more considered perspective. On top of all that, walking provides good exercise—talk about multitasking!

A perfect place to begin reading about walking is with Geoff Nicholson's delectably idiosyncratic **The Lost Art of Walking: The History, Science, Philosophy, and Literature of Pedestrianism**. (Thanks to Nicholson, I now refer to falling as "a disagreement with gravity.") You'll discover all sorts of odd tidbits of information (useful when confronted with any awkward lulls in conversations), including: Farsi has nine synonyms for walking, while Norwegian has over fifty; the idea of Velcro came to its inventor during a walk; in 1809 a British gentleman named

Robert Barclay Allardice walked one mile an hour for a thousand hours in a row and won one thousand guineas as a result; and much, much more.

A stately, wide-ranging study of the history, philosophy, and literature of walking is Rebecca Solnit's **Wanderlust**. Until I read this, I never knew that Thomas Hobbes (author of **Leviathan** and coiner of the phrase "solitary, poor, nasty, brutish, and short" to describe the life of man) had a special walking stick with an inkhorn at the top so he could jot down anything of importance that occurred to him as he was out on one of his peregrinations. Solnit's book also has a lovely series of quotations—from Virginia Wolff to Ivan Illich—running along the bottom of every page. Or it might be more fitting to say, walking along the bottom of every page.

Here are some entertaining, sometimes quirky, and often stirring accounts of individual (long) walks.

Bold Spirit: Helga Estby's Forgotten Walk Across Victorian America explores the life of an indomitable woman. In the 1890s Helga, a mother of eight children, and her eighteen-year-old daughter, Clara, walked from Spokane, Washington, to New York City in order to win a $10,000 prize and thereby save their family farm. The consequences of her journey affected her relationship with her husband, her children, and her community, all of which Linda Lawrence Hunt explores in this moving tale.

In the first week of September 2001, Tom Fremantle began following in the footsteps of Colonel Arthur Fremantle (a cousin of sorts), who traveled from the Mexico-Texas border up to New York during the summer of 1863—getting rides on stagecoaches, railroads, and riverboats. Tom decided to walk the whole way, accompanied only by a seventeen-year-old mule named Browny, and describes his trip in **The Moonshine Mule**.

Miles Away: A Walk Across France by Miles Morland describes the month he and his wife—neophyte long-distance walkers—spent trekking by foot from the Mediterranean to the Atlantic. Their story is amusing, self-deprecating, and, above all, inspiring; I can sort of imagine shouldering a backpack and following in their footsteps.

In early 1990, as the Cold War ended and cataclysmic changes were occurring all over Eastern Europe, Jason Goodwin and two friends decided to walk from Poland through Czechoslovakia, Hungary, Romania, and Bulgaria all the way to Istanbul and see how people were responding to political events along the way. The result, **On Foot to the Golden Horn: A Walk to Istanbul**, is a book that meshes armchair travel and the history of a region into a substantial yet inviting read.

And, of course, don't forget these classics: Eric Newby's ironically titled **A Short Walk in the Hindu Kush**; Henry David Thoreau's **Walking** (far less well known than **Walden**); and Peter Jenkins's **A Walk Across America**.

WATER, WATER EVERYWHERE

I was laughing pretty much all the time I was reading Terry Darlington's delightful **Narrow Dog to Indian River**. Despite their ages (seventies) and the fact that it had never been done before, Terry and his wife, Monica, leave their home in Stone, England, to take their narrowboat, *Phyllis May* (named for Terry's mother, who, though many years dead, sometimes reappears in odd places), on the 1,150-mile Intercoastal Waterway from Virginia down to the Gulf of Mexico, accompanied by their whippet, Jim. A narrowboat, as I learned, is also known as a canal boat; it's six feet, ten inches wide (Jim, the whippet, is about six inches wide) and sixty feet long (just imagine what it looks like!), with a top speed of 6.2 miles per hour. It's perfect for cruising the canals of Europe, but perhaps not so great for the open water that the Darlingtons need to contend with on their journey. Nonetheless the trio set out, encountering ice storms; high seas; piranhas; chiggers; the Southern phenomena of sweet tea, grits, and good ole boys and their families; and lots of that hospitality the region is known for. Terry relates all of the adventures in hilarious vignettes. While I don't think I'm brave enough to ever duplicate the trip the Darlingtons made, reading this made me think about (a) getting a whippet and (b) taking a narrowboat trip through the canals in England. (If you enjoyed Darlington's book as much as I did, check out his first, **Narrow Dog to Carcassonne**, which is equally fun to read.)

And if you find that reading humorous books about cruising is just your cup of tea, definitely try to find the pleasurable memoirs of Emily Kimbrough, mostly published between the 1950s and the early 1970s, including **And a Right Good Crew** (canals of England; interestingly enough, she and her travel companions begin their journey in the town where the Darlingtons live); **Water, Water Everywhere** (Greek Islands); **Time Enough** (Ireland); **Floating Island**; and **Better Than Oceans**. I spent many lovely hours rereading these—I do wish someone would republish them. They're a delightful look back at a sort of travel best described, perhaps, as "comfortable," when you dress for dinner and have cocktails when the sun is over the yardarm (whatever that means), written by someone who's not afraid to laugh fondly at herself or her friends.

Because I have an abiding interest in anything about New Zealand, I just gobbled down **Southern Exposure: A Solo Sea Kayaking Journey Around New Zealand's South Island**. I was glad to be along for the ride, and yet still remain dry enough to keep reading.

Other waterlogged books include Keith Bowden's description of a potentially dangerous and always fascinating journey by canoe, bicycle, and raft in **The Tecate Journals: Seventy Days on the Rio Grande**. Bowden offers some nice words about the American Border Patrol agents whom he meets along the way. Here's the first sentence of the book: "When I first glimpsed the Rio Grande, I mistook it for a sewer drain."

And still more: In **Rivergods: Exploring the World's Great Wild Rivers**, Richard Bangs and Christian Kallen detail their raft trips on rivers from the Apurimac (Peru) to the Zambezi (Zambia); Jonathan Raban describes his journey around England in his boat *Gosfield Maid* in **Coasting: A Private Voyage**, and a later trip down the Mississippi in **Old Glory**; **Descending the Dragon: My Journey Down the Coast of Vietnam** by Jon Bowermaster contains superb photographs by Rob Howard; and former *New York Times* Asia correspondent Edward A. Gargan tells his story in **The River's Tale: A Year on the Mekong**. Here's a quote from Gargan that I was especially taken with:

> Rivers are inherently interesting, both as geo-graphical phenomena and as metaphors for larger

questions. They mold landscapes, sunder them with gaping canyons, nurture inland fisheries, lavish the bounty of the lands they travel through into vast fertile deltas.

WE'LL ALWAYS HAVE PARIS

Let's face it—foreigners will nearly always feel like outsiders in Paris. Still, this does not stop readers (and visitors) from wanting to experience the beauty of the City of Light. Whether one enters the world of Paris through the artistry of Henry James, Edith Wharton, and Ernest Hemingway, or through the stories and novels of contemporary authors, any reader can vicariously appreciate the magic of this city.

One way to best get a sense of Paris is to understand its (and France's) history. If you want to meet the most interesting and charismatic woman of whom you've probably never heard, one whose life intersected with most of the famous people in a turbulent time in French history—everyone from Robespierre to Napoleon—read **Dancing to the Precipice: The Life of Lucie de la Tour du Pin, Eyewitness to an Era** by Caroline Moorehead.

Of course one siren song that brings people to Paris is French cuisine. Julia Child's memoir **My Life in France** (co-written with her nephew, Alex Prud'homme) captures this dual fascination with the city and its gustatory delights. An even more recent entry in the Paris-equals-good-food experience is Kathleen Flinn's **The Sharper Your Knife, the Less You Cry**. The author attended Julia Child's alma mater, Le Cordon Bleu, and while lovingly describing the markets and streets of Paris, invokes both the joy and terror of being a student at this famous school.

In **A Corner in the Marais: Memoir of a Paris Neighborhood**, Alex Karmel attempts something different. By following the historical record surrounding a centuries-old building in one of the most charming districts of the city, Karmel creates a window back in time for those of us who always wonder—who walked down these streets, and what happened here? Anyone planning to stay in this lovely quarter of Paris shouldn't miss this book.

Adam Gopnik's memoir **Paris to the Moon** provides what I believe is the best insight into the Paris that most people dream about. Gopnik spent five years living there with his wife and infant son, and he manages to make the city and its people seem at once both frustrating and captivating, bringing them as close to the truth that an outsider can most likely experience.

I've always believed that one of the best ways to find out about a place or a time period is through reading children's fiction, and Gopnik's **The King in the Window** made French history, and the city of Paris, so real to me. I highly recommend this fantasy novel aimed at young teens (but enjoyable for adult readers as well) to everyone I know who's headed there.

Time Was Soft There is Jeremy Mercer's memoir of living in an apartment above, and working for, the famed Paris bookstore Shakespeare & Co.

Gillian Tindall's **Footprints in Paris: A Few Streets, A Few Lives** showcases her uncanny ability to make a place (and the past) live again through the evocation of the people who wandered its streets, stopped in its shops, and worshipped at its churches. In this book, she explores the life of a family—her family, in fact—over two centuries, living on the Left Bank of Paris.

By using the writer's imagination to invoke a sense of place, a work of fiction presents a different view of Paris. In **Suite Française** Irène Némirovsky paints a portrait of the City of Light awaiting the darkness to come. Even though the novel quickly moves away from Paris, its stark portrayal of a world about to be lost remains powerful.

In Alan Furst's **The World at Night**, darkness has indeed descended over Paris after its occupation by Hitler's forces. Furst's tale of a reluctant, unintentional secret agent trying to stay alive in the shifting sands of the occupied city mirrors the black and white tone of films from that era.

Dark images still can exist in the contemporary City of Light, especially in the novels of Cara Black. The author has written a number of mysteries set in the many different neighborhoods of Paris. In **Murder in Belleville** she creates a tension-filled portrait of the historic Arab district, as private investigator Aimée Leduc follows a case involving the deportation of illegal immigrants.

Graham Robb's **Parisians: An Adventure History of Paris** conjures up events of the Parisian past in the lives of men and women from Marie Antoinette to Charles Baudelaire. Robb is also the author of **The Discovery of France: A Historical Geography**.

Finally, two recent novels by French authors show us that Parisian apartment buildings can be worlds in themselves. In **Hunting and Gathering** Anna Gavalda charms us with a story of disparate misfits who share a barely furnished apartment in a grand old building. And Muriel Barbery's **The Elegance of the Hedgehog** offers us the story of a young girl's friendship with the elderly concierge in her apartment building and reminds us that even Parisians can feel like outsiders in their own city.

WHERE IN THE WORLD DO THESE BOOKS BELONG?

Quite often as I was doing all the reading in preparation for writing this book, I'd come across a book that I thought would be perfect, only to realize that there was no easy way to categorize it. It didn't fit comfortably anywhere, but clearly belonged somewhere because I enjoyed it so much, wanted many others to read it, and it was at least minimally connected to travel. See what you think of these.

To read **The Clumsiest People in Europe, Or: Mrs. Mortimer's Bad-Tempered Guide to the Victorian World** is to get a picture of a particular mid-nineteenth-century English mind—one that is didactic, horribly prejudiced, and a believer in the absolute correctness of the English way of life as well as the enormous benefits conferred by being a member of the British Empire. I must say that I winced even as I smiled at Mrs. Mortimer's comparisons of the "uncivilized" peoples of the world with those "civilized" people fortunate enough to be residing in that sunniest (maybe not literally), most advanced, happiest, and most fortunate of locales: England. Todd Pruzan's first-rate introduction puts Mrs. Mortimer's beliefs into context.

George R. Stewart's **Names on the Land: A Historical Account of Place-Naming in the United States** is one of those rare biblio-animals: a pleasure to read that brings along with it a lot of interesting information to drop into conversational lulls at cocktail or dinner parties. Why is it Arkansas and not Arkansaw? What are the historical reasons for a Warsaw in Indiana, one in Virginia, and one in Georgia? Stewart tells us all this, and more.

I cannot adequately convey how much I absolutely adored Vivian Swift's **When Wanderers Cease to Roam: A Traveler's Journal of Staying Put**. For over two decades Swift traveled the world for work and fun, and then settled down with five cats in a house in a small village on Long Island Sound. This is a diary (highly illustrated with her watercolor drawings) of those years, as well as the events of her past. It's totally enchanting.

It's through Swift's book that I learned about the mid-eighteenth-century writer Xavier de Maistre, who was under house arrest (for dueling) and decided to write about the items in his room as though they were important tourist attractions, in **Voyage Around My Room**. Swift says that he "invented a new mode of travel." I love that description.

Other odd and rather wonderful more-or-less armchair travel books (or at least books about travel), include these:

Caroline Alexander writes winningly about all the places that influenced Coleridge's famous poem, "Kubla Khan" in **The Way to Xanadu**.

Frederick Burnaby journeyed alone from London's Victoria Station to Central Asia in 1875. His adventures are described in **A Ride to Khiva**—a classic book of armchair travel that was originally published in 1876 (and reprinted eleven times in the first year it came out). All authors should be so fortunate!

Like all of Alain de Botton's books—whether his subject is Proust or, as here, musings and anecdotes on traveling—in **The Art of Travel** you'll find both delightful writing and lots of observations to mull over.

Barbara Crossette's **The Great Hill Stations of Asia** describes those towns—some built more than two centuries ago—that the Europeans constructed in foreign climes in order to relax, leave the heat of the cities on the plains, and escape what came to be known as "tropical fatigue." As Crossette points out, many of these are still lovely places to visit.

From 1924 to 1939 (when he is to believed to have died in a typhoon while sailing a Chinese junk from Hong Kong to San Francisco), Richard Halliburton traveled the world and wrote about his experiences in first-person, you-are-there prose. His books—filled with adventure and a wee bit dated now—include **The Royal Road to Romance**, **The Glorious Adventure**, **New Worlds to Conquer**, **Seven League Boots**, and **The Flying Carpet**.

Tété-Michel Kpomassie's **An African in Greenland** tells the wondrous tale of a teenager whose imagination was captured by reading a book on Greenland, and who slowly worked his way north from his home in Africa's tropical Togoland to fulfill his dream of one day living there.

Robert Macfarlane's **The Wild Places** is set in Ireland and England; the places he describes include beaches, salt marshes, forests, and other locales not yet invaded and despoiled by people. Poetic, thoughtful, and sure to lead readers to a desire for silence and—perhaps—a solitary journey of their own.

In **Pagan Holiday: On the Trail of Ancient Roman Tourists**, author Tony Perrottet had a splendid idea: to retrace the travels of ancient Romans as they ventured throughout their Empire from Pompeii to Egypt and beyond. As he follows in their footsteps two thousand years or so later, Perrottet makes apt comparisons between the ancient cities and their contemporary counterparts, all the while interspersing delightfully prophetic quotes from ancient travelers. (The book is sometimes found under the title **Route 66 A.D.: On the Trail of Ancient Roman Tourists**.)

In 1926 Vita Sackville-West went out to visit her diplomat husband, who was stationed in Iran. In **Passenger to Teheran** she describes a leisurely journey—via boat, train, and automobiles. She's scrupulous in her descriptions and honest in her appraisal of the places she visited. (She hated India and admired Isfahan, for example.)

Mark Twain's **The Innocents Abroad** is essential reading if you need a laugh and want to get a feel for American attitudes in the years right after the Civil War. The travelers Twain describes are probably the first "ugly Americans," so this is not the book to read if you're particularly touchy about criticism or if political correctness is extremely important to you. Here's one of my favorite lines: "When I think of how I have been swindled by books of Oriental travel, I want a tourist for breakfast."

The title of Mo Willems's book seems to say it all: **You Can Never Find a Rickshaw When It Monsoons: The World on One Cartoon a Day**.

Simon Winchester's **Outposts: Journeys to the Surviving Relics of the British Empire** was originally published as **The Sun Never Sets: Travels to the Remaining Outposts of the British Empire**; whatever its title, it is a pleasure to read.

In David Yeadon's **The Back of Beyond: Travels to the Wild Places of the Earth**, he seeks out the places where tourists seldom go. He's a wonderful companion—friendly and unflappable, and always eager to discover more. One thing to remember when you read this: it was published in 1991, and many of the places he writes about are no longer at the back of beyond—they've since been discovered by the rest of the world, like Nepal's Kathmandu.

I know where Christopher Robbins's **Apples Are from Kazakhstan: The Land That Disappeared** should go—in a section on the "'Stans," those former Soviet appendages. But I couldn't find enough other books that I enjoyed as much to make a section out of the topic, so I've put it here.

Both the sort of traveling (extensive) and writing (excellent) that Bruce Chatwin did are on fine display in **What Am I Doing Here** and **Far Journeys**.

WY EVER NOT?

I'm not sure why there's so much good writing set in Wyoming, by Wyoming writers, or both. Maybe it's the beauty of the Tetons and the Bighorns, the seventy-five-mile-per-hour speed limit on the lightly traveled interstates, or the seeming infinity of pure emptiness between towns. Or maybe it's just something in the water. Why ever it is, readers are able to reap the benefits of these books.

In **The Daily Coyote**, Shreve Stockton describes how she gave up her successful, highly urban life after stopping for a night in Wyoming on a cross-country trip via her 150cc Vespa ET4. Soon thereafter she left New York, rented a house sight-unseen in Ten Sleep, Wyoming, and then was given a baby coyote. Here's how she describes what captured her heart about the state:

> The landscape around the Bighorns is like an ocean on pause, rolling with the subtle colors of rust and sage and gold, stretching to every horizon. These mountains are unlike other mountain ranges. While the Tetons are fangs of stone and Rainier is an ice cream sundae, the Bighorns are sloped and subtle, built of some of the oldest exposed rock in the world; rock that has existed, in its current form, for over three billion years. There is exquisite power in their permanence.

Ron Carlson's **The Signal** is a tale of love gone wrong, a good man who made a bad mistake, and the way real evil can show up in our lives. After I read this beautifully written novel, I wanted to see the place where it took place—the Wind River Mountains in western Wyoming—for myself. I have to add, though, that I wouldn't like to go through the travails the characters did.

Margaret Coel's series of mysteries all take place on the Wind River Reservation, and all feature a priest named Father John O'Malley and a lawyer named Vicky Holden. As Tony Hillerman brings the history and traditions of the Navajos to readers, Coel does so for the Arapaho tribe. In one of my favorites, **Eye of the Wolf**, Father John and Vicky need to puzzle out whether a nineteenth-century massacre promulgated by the Shoshones on the Arapaho is at the heart of three present-day killings of three young Shoshones.

In fact, anyone looking for mysteries set in Wyoming is in for a real treat, because in addition to Coel there are also the books written by C. J. Box and Craig Johnson. Box's main character is game warden Joe Pickett. My favorite of his is **Free Fire**, but they're all filled with crisp dialogue, brisk pacing, and a main character who is satisfyingly complex. Johnson's thrillers, all set near the Bighorn Mountains, feature sheriff Walt Longmire. As good as the first book in the series (**The Cold Dish**) was—and it was very good—Johnson just keeps getting better and better with each novel. As I write this, his newest is **Junkyard Dogs**, and it's just terrific. Don't miss **The Dark Horse**, either. (You can watch my interview with Johnson at www .seattlechannel.org/videos/video.asp?ID=3030910.)

Annie Proulx has written three collections of stories set in Wyoming (known collectively, and sensibly, as "The Wyoming Stories"). They include **Close Range**, **Bad Dirt**, and **Fine Just the Way It Is**. Her most famous story is, of course, "Brokeback Mountain," which was later adapted into a superb movie. But reading these three collections together gives you an idea of her great range and stellar talent. What an amazing writer she is.

"Clever" novels frequently put me off. You know the sort I mean: those that make use of different fonts, footnotes, and other similar affectations. I often wonder if the purpose of all these bells and whistles is simply to disguise the fact that the author really has nothing much to say to the reader. And I find that so often novels about child geniuses all follow the same story arc: kid burns out and comes to no good end. So you can imagine my relief and readerly joy when I discovered that Reif Larsen overcame both of my ingrained prejudices in **The Selected Works of T. S. Spivet**. It's about twelve-year-old cartography genius Tecumseh Sparrow Spivet, who lives at the Coppertop Ranch (just north of Divide, Montana) with his über-laconic rancher father, his scientist mother (who is obsessed with finding a certain type of beetle that nobody else believes exists), his older sister, Gracie, and the memory of his younger brother, Layton, whose death has left an unhealed scar on the family's psyche. In this satisfying first novel, we experience the world through the eyes of this brilliant, funny, and emotionally wounded kid.

Other Wyoming books include a classic: Owen Wister's 1902 **The Virginian** (really, still *the* classic novel of the Wyoming territory, if not the whole West); Mark Spragg's memoir **Where Rivers Change Directions**; Gretel Ehrlich's **The Solace of Open Spaces**, with its deep appreciation of nature; and **Wyoming Summer** by Mary O'Hara, which, despite its title, isn't totally set in Wyoming, but the small sections that are really make us feel as though we're there with the author and her husband experiencing the sudden weather changes, the way the sky appears different from one moment to the next, and the tenuousness of small ranch-holdings. (O'Hara published her hit novel **My Friend Flicka**, set in a remote area of Wyoming, in 1941. **Wyoming Summer**, made up of a series of journal notes she'd been keeping, wasn't published until 1963, but she tells us that the manuscript was finished and put away long before Flicka became popular.) Here's how she describes the Wyoming sky:

> Over all, and low above me, was a pale blue sky, calm and benign. On it, flat sheets of cloud, with indeterminate, melting edges, floated so slowly, so indifferently, so serenely that they made me feel slow, indifferent and serene too.

And here:

> Now the day is waning and the light changing for sunset. Soft and lovely. No clouds. Just a clear emerald green—and the evening star big and golden.

Fabulous.

ZAMBIA

After much turmoil in the southern part of the African continent, the country of Zambia was formed out of the former Northern Rhodesia and became the Republic of Zambia in October 1964. Its existence was complicated by the fact that three of its neighbors were still under colonial powers (Southern Rhodesia, Mozambique, and Angola). Here are some books I've enjoyed over the years.

The Swedish writer Henning Mankell's novel **The Eye of the Leopard** takes place in Zambia, just after it achieved independence.

In **Scribbling the Cat**, Alexandra Fuller describes her friendship and travels in Zambia with one of her parents' neighbors, a white African and veteran of the Rhodesian Wars, both of them trying to understand the past and its attendant horrors.

Christina Lamb's **The Africa House** is a biography of Stewart Gore-Browne, a fascinating Edwardian Englishman whose contradictory attitudes toward his adopted country—Northern Rhodesia—make for fascinating reading. This is a good choice for fans of **White Mischief** by James Fox.

In **The Eye of the Elephant: An Epic Adventure in the African Wilderness**, biologists Delia and Mark Owens discuss their attempts to save Zambia's elephants from wholesale slaughter in the Luangwa Valley. (The couple was expelled from Botswana after writing **Cry of the Kalahari** and chose to settle in Zambia as a result.)

The farm in Zambia that Sheila Siddle and her husband, David, purchased became the Chimfunshi Wildlife Orphanage, the largest primate sanctuary in the world. Their adventures with their "guests" are winningly described in **In My Family Tree: A Life with Chimpanzees**.

If you're looking for much lighter fare, Mrs. Pollifax, a CIA agent in her spare time, sets out on an African safari in order to save the life of the president of Zambia, in **Mrs. Pollifax on Safari** by Dorothy Gilman. Reading this, you can't escape the feeling that Gilman herself had just been on safari, too, though the rest of the story is surely pure fiction!

ZIPPING THROUGH ZIMBABWE/
ROAMING RHODESIA

Zimbabwe, formerly Southern Rhodesia, has long been the subject of some terrific novels and memoirs—perhaps the lure for writers is its uniquely African combination of beauty and inept (and corrupt) governments that consistently fail to improve the lives of their citizens.

Journalist Peter Godwin wrote two books about growing up in Zimbabwe, and both do a remarkable job of combining the personal and the historical. Although I found **Mukiwa: A White Boy in Africa** to be engrossing and enlightening—it's set from 1964 to 1982 against the background of the war that gained Rhodesia independence and black rule as the country of Zimbabwe—I was totally hooked by the evocative writing of **When a Crocodile Eats the Sun**, which describes the long reign of Zimbabwe president Robert Mugabe in all its brutal details while at the same time exploring the repercussions of a long-held Godwin family secret.

Here are some other books—both fiction and nonfiction—that I've found engrossing since I wrote the "Dreaming of Africa" section in *Book Lust*.

> Petina Gappah's **An Elegy for Easterly: Stories**
> Wendy Kann's **Casting with a Fragile Thread: A Story of Sisters and Africa** makes a good companion read with Alexandra Fuller's **Don't Let's Go to the Dogs Tonight**.

Doris Lessing's **Under My Skin: Volume One of My Autobiography, to 1949** and **African Laughter: Four Visits to Zimbabwe**

Andrew Meldrum's **Where We Have Hope: A Memoir of Zimbabwe**

Tudor Parfitt's **Journey to the Vanished City: The Search for a Lost Tribe of Israel** (absolutely fascinating for history buffs or those interested in the history of religion)

Douglas Rogers's **The Last Resort: A Memoir of Zimbabwe**

Irene Sabatini's **The Boy Next Door**

Lauren St. John's **Rainbow's End: A Memoir of Childhood, War, and an African Farm**

Wilbur Smith's Ballantyne series are perfect airplane reads, while at the same time offering a pretty accurate account of historical events. You'll probably want to read them in order: **A Falcon Flies**, **Men of Men**, **The Angels Weep**, and **The Leopard Hunts in Darkness**. (Smith has written over thirty books set in Africa, so if you fall in love with reading about the continent, he's an author you'll want to remember.)

Yvonne Vera's painful-to-read novel **The Stone Virgins** describes the lives of sisters Thenjiwe and Nonceba living during the period when Zimbabwe gained independence from Britain.

INDEX

Note: **Bold text** refers to book and series titles.